CW00705750

# WOMEN, MEN &
# RAPE

# WOMEN, MEN &
# RAPE

**Ray Wyre & Anthony Swift**

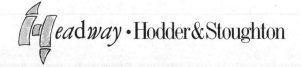
Headway · Hodder & Stoughton

© 1990 Ray Wyre & Anthony Swift

First published in Great Britain in 1990

*British Library Cataloguing in Publication Data*
Wyre, Ray
    Women, men & rape.
    1. Crimes. Rape
    I. Title   II. Swift, Anthony
    364.1532

    ISBN 0 340 52924 5

All rights reserved. No part of this publication may be reproduced
or transmitted in any form or by any means, electronically or
mechanically, including photocopying, recording or any information
storage or retrieval system, without either the prior permission in
writing from the publisher or a licence permitting restricted copying.
In the United Kingdom such licences are issued by the Copyright
Licensing Agency, 33–34 Alfred Place, London WC1E 7DP.

Phototypeset by Input Typesetting Ltd, London
Printed in Great Britain for the educational publishing division of
Hodder and Stoughton Ltd, Mill Road, Dunton Green, Sevenoaks,
Kent by Richard Clay Ltd, Bungay, Suffolk.

*For Shirley, Tim, Matthew and Rebecca*
*Annie and Annatjie*

# CONTENTS

About the Authors                                      ix

Note to the Reader                                     xi

**1**  Attack and response                              1
**2**  Types of sex attacker                            9
**3**  The rape process                                19
**4**  The rape and sexual assault of children         37
**5**  Obscene phone calls                             55
**6**  Public action                                   63

Notes and References                                   77

# ABOUT
# THE AUTHORS

**Ray Wyre** is well known for his pioneering work in promoting the treatment of male sex offenders in the UK. He heads a multi-disciplinary team running a treatment programme at the Gracewell Clinic, near Birmingham, of which he is a founder–director. Gracewell is Britain's first residential clinic for child sex abusers.

Formerly, as a Probation Officer with the Hampshire Probation Service, Ray Wyre designed and for four years ran an extensive treatment programme for rapists and other sex offenders held in one of Her Majesty's prisons. The insights in this book into the thoughts and actions of sex offenders are drawn from his knowledge of the field and his many years of counselling, directing treatment programmes and conducting group therapy work with such men.

In 1984 Ray Wyre was awarded a Churchill Fellowship to study the treatment of offenders and victims, and police procedure in investigating sex crimes in the United States. He believes that imprisonment without treatment followed by the release of such offenders into the community serves to increase the severity of attacks on women. He is much in demand as a speaker at seminars and conferences concerning sex offences and child abuse, runs training courses and is frequently consulted by the media.

**Anthony Swift**, a freelance journalist and writer, has contributed many ideas and helped to plan and develop the themes of the book and has been largely responsible for writing it in close collaboration with Ray Wyre. As a journalist, for many years in South Africa, he has specialised in writing about child abuse and other social and racial issues. He is co-author of *Broken Promise – The World of Endangered Children* (Headway 1989).

# NOTE
# TO THE READER

In 1988, nearly 3000 women in Britain reported to the police that they had been raped – an increase of 16 per cent – and in all 26 529 sex crimes were recorded. But the recorded incidence hides rather than reveals the enormity of the situation because, as is well known, most women who suffer these appalling experiences do not report them.

In the United States it has been estimated that only between one in four and one in ten rapes are reported.[1] A possible indicator in the UK is that 75 per cent of the women who approach the London Rape Crisis for help do not go on to tell the police of the crimes committed against them. A recent survey by *Company* magazine of its readers found that ten per cent of the women respondents had experienced assault, or actual or attempted rape, but only three per cent had reported it to the police.[2] If one includes the unreported incidence of other sexual abuses of women – which may be as psychologically destructive as rape – as well as the sexual abuse of children, this kind of violence must be far more commonplace in our culture than we generally recognise.

In counselling sessions, seminars and group work, it is

common for women to confide for the first time about offences they have never reported, often committed against them when they were children.

From the offenders' side of the story, numerous convicts have revealed in counselling sessions that they committed many offences which were never investigated. Most had successfully given the impression during police investigations and court hearings that their offences were one-off events. One man confessed to three or four indecent assaults a week. He had just started to rape when he was caught. Mark said that he had attacked women for more than two years before he was convicted of rape. His main motive was to inspire fear.

The New York Psychiatric Institute, which specialises in the treatment of sex offenders, finds that on average rapists strike 7.5 times. But there is evidence of a higher ratio than this; 53 sex offenders treated at the Oregon State Hospital in the US had committed 25 757 sexual crimes.[3]

The incidence of rape is likely to continue to rise until the authorities make it a priority to support efforts to offer treatment as part of the sentencing of offenders and their subsequent return to the community, and until there is a greater commitment to understanding the social and psychological roots of this type of violence.

This book is offered in diffident awareness that increasingly women are resistant to being told by men how to perceive and think about their lives. How can male authors presume to produce a book that partly considers the response of women to rape? The answer is that this book is mainly about men – the sort of men who sexually attack women, though it also looks at the often devastating impact of such attacks on the women who survive them.

Based extensively on the accounts of offenders undergoing treatment in and outside prison, it hopes to provide some insight into how they think about and plan their attacks, how they draw on ideas prevalent in society to justify what they do and how they are affected by the way women respond to their attacks.

It is not intended to be prescriptive though some straight

advice is offered. What it does is:

- Show that, though rape is always a life-threatening experience, there are different types of sex offender – some of whom are less dangerous than others and more likely to be put off by various reactions of their victims.
- Assert that rape is not a spontaneous act committed by a man in the grip of an uncontrollable sexual urge but is more often a much-rehearsed and fantasised attempt to wield power over another person.
- Argue that rape is not a single violent event whose conclusion is decided by the victory or loss of an initial physical struggle. It is a complex mental, emotional and physical process in which, at every stage, the survivor can hope to retain some measure of control.
- Suggest that women's psychological and emotional reactions might help them exercise control more effectively than simple physical self-defence training.
- Identify potential reforms in the treatment of sex offenders that might help reduce the incidence of rape.

The ideas are offered in the hope that, by exploring how male sex offenders think and act, women may increase their awareness of the nature of the threat against them and be better equipped in the event of an attack, and men may discover how inappropriate certain commonly accepted attitudes about women and about rape are.

Most of the information in this book is derived from sex offenders in the UK and other countries who have volunteered to take part in treatment designed to offer them controls over their behaviour and make them less of a danger to the community. It also draws on the accounts of men referred by voluntary and statutory agencies for assessment and individuals seeking counselling for sexual problems, interviews with prisoners in the United States, as well as information supplied by other therapists and treatment centres, by Rape Crisis and some of the survivors of sexual assault.

Descriptions of the experiences of individuals are disguised to make identification impossible. Similarities to any person are coincidental. Some of the incidents described and language used may disturb some readers but we felt it would be unhelpful to disguise the very real aggression of some sexual attacks.

Thanks are due to the Hampshire Probation Service, which encouraged the development of a prison-based treatment programme for sex offenders; to Charles Fortt, formerly a Probation Officer in Suffolk, now with Gracewell; Dr Arnon Bentovim of the Great Ormond Street Children's Hospital; the Winston Churchill Memorial Trust, and former colleagues of Ray Wyre in the Probation Service. We also want to thank Diana Warren-Holland, a rape survivor and now a counsellor with Portsmouth Rape Crisis, who gave valuable feed-back in the preparation of, and wrote a foreword to, the first edition of this book. Ann Perry cast an editorial eye over the draft manuscript and made many useful suggestions.

There are substantial changes in this edition. There are more examples of offender behaviour and thinking, a new section on obscene phone callers and the chapters on the rape and sexual abuse of children and public attitudes have been considerably strengthened.

This book is the result of a fruitful and stimulating collaboration. Many interesting ideas emerged in the course of writing it. However, co-authorship is inevitably something of a three-legged journey at times. Where it is necessary to define a statement as deriving from one of us (usually relating to offender behaviour) we have used the phrase 'the author'.

This is not a book on how to handle rape. Many survivors of rape blame themselves and feel they have failed society's expectations by not having fought their attackers harder. While we hope to stimulate interest in the non-physical aspects of resistance to rape, as well as help women understand men who rape and so perhaps better survive their actions, the last effect we want is to create new fertile areas of guilt and self-doubt by suggesting new ways to respond to rape attack which the reader then finds she is unable to apply.

*Ray Wyre and Anthony Swift, August 1989*

# O N E

---

# ATTACK
# AND RESPONSE

Not all sexual attacks on women end up as the attackers plan.
What victims happen to say and do can dramatically affect the
course of events.

A man, who had a history of indecent assault and rape,
attacked a woman in a car park. He threatened her with a knife
and put a bag over her head. He forced her to undress, tearing
some of her clothes off. 'I said I was going to rape her. She could
have shouted her head off. Nobody would have heard. She was
talking to me. As I forced her to the floor she said: "Do you
know God loves you just as much as He loves me." I don't know
why, I just turned and ran.'

Another convicted rapist had a history in adolescence of putting his hands up girls' skirts in playgrounds. He went on to
making obscene phone calls and fantasised frequently about
taking a woman by force. He always imagined his victim would
respond favourably to the macho presentation he saw himself as
making by his attack on her and that she would begin to take
the dominant role.

One night he surprised a young woman. He grabbed her from
behind and ordered her to undress. 'I thought she'd be terrified.

She said firmly: "Leave my clothing alone. I will not be used by you." I panicked and ran off.'

Accounts, by both survivors and offenders, of attacks that have been abandoned reveal a wide variety of responses that have deterred attackers. A study in the United States identified the following.[4]

- Verbal counter-attack – 'You bastard. Get your fucking hands off me'.
- Physical attack – kicking and punching.
- Feigning body weakness – 'I'm expecting a baby'/'I've got cancer of the womb'.
- Virginity – 'I'm about to get married and want to remain a virgin'.
- Moral appeal – 'This is against God's command. It will be wrong to rape me'.
- Interpersonal – 'My name is Mary. Why do you want to do this to me? I'm just a person like you'.
- Self-punitive – 'I'll never get over this. You will make me have a mental breakdown'.
- Retribution – 'You will be caught for this and go to jail'.
- Ambivalence – alternately fighting and giving up the fight.
- Acquiescence – offering no resistance at all.

Not enough is known about the cases from which these examples are taken, or about the individuals involved, to provide a clear object lesson in how to handle a rape situation. Because we are all different and every attack is different, such a guideline is probably not even possible, though clearly a more systematic collection of information, both from victims and offenders, would be helpful. What these examples do establish is that non-violent responses to sexual attack have, by luck or intuition, effectively dissuaded some attackers. Rape is not a foregone conclusion at the onset of an attack. A study of 915 rapes and attempted rapes showed that some 300 had been thwarted – more than 200 of these as a result of something the victim said or did.[5]

Nevertheless, whatever the degree of violence used, rape is

intrinsically a violent and life-threatening experience. Many women subjected to it find themselves totally debilitated by fear.

Perhaps understandably, too much emphasis has been placed on the physical aspects both of the attack and the victim's response. In some societies there is a social expectation that women should effectively resist being raped or shoulder part of the blame. It would seem to be implicit, for instance, in the Code of Hammurabi under Babylonian law – 4000 years ago – whereby if a married woman was subjected to rape, both she and the rapist were bound together and thrown into a river to die. In more recent times, for rape to be established in some states of America it has been necessary in law for the woman to prove she physically resisted her attackers (an attitude hardly calculated to stimulate the reporting of rape).

Courses in physical self-defence are still the most commonly suggested preparation against a rape attack and they may incidentally contribute to the climate of opinion that it is morally wrong not to fight off a rape attack.

The question of whether a woman should attempt physical retaliation against a male attacker is commonly raised. A simple yes/no answer is likely to be both unhelpful and unrealistic. Each person must judge for themselves how best to respond to life-threatening events and they may reasonably make very different decisions in differing circumstances. It is a survival and not a moral issue.

In contradiction of the rape validation requirements of some American states just noted, the FBI in New York was so alarmed by the growing incidence of injury to women during sexual attacks a few years back that they distributed a poster warning against confrontational forms of response to rapists.[6]

An argument in favour of physical defence courses has been that they increase the confidence with which women present themselves in public and this may deter men who avoid attacking confident-looking women. However, though many rapists do have quite specific ideas about the type of woman they target, some pick on women who display social confidence.

Another problem with an over-emphasis on physical self-defence is that it may provide both a false sense of security and a barrier to the exploration of alternative, or additional and perhaps safer defensive strategies.

Terrifying situations are difficult if not impossible to simulate. The extreme violence and aggression of some rapists is hard to imagine unless you have actually been exposed to it and is likely to overwhelm the physical confidence of all but the most accomplished or lucky of unarmed combat experts. Physical defence courses for women have shifted in emphasis towards enabling them to create opportunities to escape rather than attack. However, someone who relies exclusively on physical defence could find themselves quickly at a loss and with no other resources to fall back on.

The following paragraph describes a level of violence not uncommon in certain kinds of rape. If you feel it will be likely only to increase your fear levels without being helpful to you then skip the lines in italics.

*Alex abducted a young woman to a derelict block of flats. He tore her clothes off her, swearing, and cursing her. He threatened her with a knife and made superficial cuts on her face. He took off his belt and whipped her viciously with the buckle end. He then placed the hilt end of the knife in her vagina and said he would put the sharp end in if she did not do what he told her. He sodomised her and then forced her to have oral sex. He swung through huge changes of mood. At one time he apologised and told the young woman she could leave, only to drag her back after she had dressed and put her through the whole life-threatening ordeal again.*

Basically, in a rape attack anything one might imagine in the way of abuse and bestiality is possible. A recurring theme of rapists' accounts of their actions is that they have no value for themselves. Their life experience has given them no sense of being wanted or needed and they are on a 'self-destruct' course, some of them determined to take what they can of the world with them. Against such angry men, a violent response by the victim may well only trigger increased levels of violence. If the victim of the attack described by Alex had offered counter-violence she would have greatly increased her chances of being killed.

Even rape involving minimal physical force is experienced by the victim as life-threatening in that the woman is robbed of control over her body by someone whose capability for violence she knows little or nothing about. At no stage can she be sure about what will happen next.

Rape should not be equated simply with forms of common physical assault, because it specifically attacks a woman's sexuality, a primary means of experiencing and expressing love, caring and gentleness. But it is worth noting that very few men, who are socialised – and often trained – to be physically combative, retaliate when challenged by a physically violent assailant. According to a television documentary on street crime, only one man in ten offers any resistance at all when mugged. The fact is, if you freeze in the face of violence you are just behaving like most people do.

The very idea of physically taking on a more powerful or desperate aggressor may intensify some victims' level of terror, contributing to the total freeze syndrome so many survivors of rape have reported.

If the idea of fighting off a rapist does raise the victim's fear to a point where it blocks her resourcefulness and deprives her of any chance of exercising some control, it is clearly not a useful option. The victim's fear does nothing to deter rapists generally and may positively encourage some. Such are the rationalising powers of rapists that fighting back physically may not even be the best way of making your attitude known. Some rapists choose to believe that women try to fight them off physically to assuage feelings of guilt about having sex with them and to be able to justify the sexual encounter later to a husband or boyfriend. Chris, who raped a neighbour, claimed it was not rape, because after an initial physical struggle his victim submitted without any further verbal or physical opposition.

Rapists express surprise that most of their victims submit with little or no verbal protest, sometimes after a brief physical struggle. It would seem from their accounts that, apart from those women who freeze with fear, many others appear cool and composed. They may say, 'Please don't', or 'Don't hurt me' but without much conviction or anger. This apparent coolness is to do with the psychological distancing or anaesthetising people commonly experience in life-threatening situations. Some rapists have told of having actually handed weapons to their victims and being surprised that they made no attempt to use them. One was puzzled that after he had raped a woman she meekly went with him as he moved about the house; he believed she did not want him to leave her in a room alone.

Rapists, of course, represent such incidents, and the apparent collapse of opposition from some of their victims, as proof that women do not mind being raped or that they had sex with them voluntarily. One man, dressed as a woman, surprised a woman in a public lavatory and threatened to rape her at knife-point. The woman told him: 'I'll do nothing unless you throw the knife away'. She then urged him to 'get a move on and get it over with'. He later cited this as evidence that she did not mind being raped, whereas it was clearly a successful survival strategy that will have left her some sense of control.

Another young rapist said repeatedly through his tears, during an interview preparatory to his prosecution: 'Why didn't she stop me? Why didn't she stop me? She must have known I didn't want to do it', as though it was her responsibility to save him from himself.

Until we understand more about the ways in which fear affects people, the rationalisations of offenders may gain more credence than they deserve with the police and courts. Evidence gathered from rape victims in the United States[7] shows that, of those threatened physically, 55 per cent were 'submissive', 27 per cent resisted and 18 per cent fought.

The relative lack of protest by victims of sex attacks is the most common reason given by offenders as to why they have carried through with attacks, whereas on other occasions they have abandoned them. They go through with them partly because they find it easy. If the victim offers a rapist no opposition at all – as she very well might if her only defence plan is physical and she loses confidence in it at the last minute – he will proceed to rape her.

Whatever they may feel at the time of the rape, survivors are often left with a tangle of self-destructive emotions and may be plagued years after the event by feelings of guilt about not having fought harder. Ironically, the very fact of their survival can be evidence that they acted in exactly the right way.

In commenting on the first edition of this book, Diana Warren-Holland, herself a rape victim and now a Rape Crisis counsellor, made it clear that the major impediment faced by the victim in countering her assailant was paralysis by her own fear and this could happen even where a woman believed she had prepared herself well mentally. This raises the question of what it is to prepare yourself well mentally.

It must be valuable to know that there are different types of sex attacker and that some are likely to take flight if challenged verbally. You do not need to risk repelling them physically to drive them off.

John has never experienced sexual intercourse with a mutually consenting woman. He had an early jail sentence for indecent assaults and, after listening to the accounts of other convicted rapists, resolved to rape a woman upon his release. His first victim resisted and he took to his heels. His next was clearly too frozen by fear to resist and despite some sexual dysfunction, he raped her.

John is what I define as a sexual rapist.

# TYPES OF
# SEX ATTACKER

Before we look at different types of sex attacker it is worth briefly considering two broad categories – stranger, and date-and-acquaintance rape. They refer not so much to the type of offender as the relationship between offender and victim. Stranger rape is where the rapist is unknown to the victim and generally, though not necessarily, the victim is unknown to the attacker. Some attackers target their victims well ahead of an attack. A teenager who was attacked and raped in her own home, while her parents slept in the next room, was selected by the rapist from a picture and caption in a local newspaper which identified her place of work. He followed her home and carefully planned the rape.

Stranger rapes account for most of the attacks that become sensationalised in the tabloids and result in court proceedings. The Fox, the Cambridge rapist, the M5 rapist and more recently John Cannan, the rapist and killer of Shirley Banks, are among the more notorious examples.

But far more common and less reported are date-and-acquaintance rapes. They include attacks by men who deliberately cultivate a relationship with a woman with the intention of raping her (see socio-pathic rapists below) or her children, and men who, in the context of a working or personal relationship, use physical or other power they have over a woman to induce her to yield to sexual demands.

The date-and-acquaintance rapist may pick his victim up on the night of the rape, appearing to want to form a relationship. He may see her several times before the rape occurs. He may be in a position of trust and authority over her (a boss, a counsellor or, in the case of child rape, a father or step-father). Most abuse of children by paedophiles and all cases of incest fall into this category. So would rape of a woman by a boyfriend, a partner or husband.

Date-and-acquaintance rapes are less reported for various reasons.

The victim is often less clear about whether or not she will be seen to be partly to blame.

Evidence of sexual intercourse does not, in such cases, prove rape – DNA profiling, greeted as a major breakthrough in rape investigations, has little value in the majority of rape cases where the offender is known to the victim.

Because the evidence centres on the issue of consent, police investigation and court hearings are more victim than offender focused.

The survivor in many instances does not want to break up the family. She may fear she will not be believed (many children who report having been sexually abused meet with the disbelief of family members who do not want to recognise the truth of the situation). She may fear reprisals by an offender who has some power over her – perhaps the power to hire or fire her, or pass or fail her in an exam, or eject her from the home, or perhaps straightforward physical or intellectual power; any means, in fact, that makes a person submit to sexual demands for any other reason than that she also wants a sexual relationship.

In the treatment of sex offenders it is useful to identify various types of rapist. Some of these categories are already well-established;[8] others have been found useful by the author in the course of therapeutic counselling and group work with offenders.

Among them are sexual, anger, socio-pathic, and sadistic rapists, fixated paedophiles and regressed paedophiles.

As with all typologies there is over-simplification; not all offenders fit neatly into one or another type. A considerable number who might be typed in a particular way have also committed acts not attributed to that type. In fact, the more we learn about offending the more we come across rapists of adults who also sexually abuse children on occasion, or men who rape their own wives as well as other women. The targeting of single-parent families by paedophiles is blurring the distinction between incest and the abuse of children outside the family.

Prison experience shows that one 'type' of offender may develop the practices of other types. Convicted rapists who had never used implements (sticks or bottles) have begun to build their use into their sexual fantasies after talking with other rapists in prison.

Despite these discrepancies, the differences are sufficiently distinguishable to make the typology valuable in the therapeutic counselling of offenders, particularly in getting them to talk. Recognition that an offender belongs to a certain type enables the counsellor to show that he knows the offender behaves in certain ways and that gives the offender 'permission' to talk.

The typology may also be of use to the victims of rape attack, and to the police. It may help the rape survivor identify more about the person she is having to contend with and so give her more opportunity to exercise some control, and it should greatly assist the identification and capture of offenders.

It has become almost a cliché that rape is not to do with sex but with anger and power. And rape clearly is an attempt to exercise power over another individual, though the impulse is often born of an acute sense of powerlessness.

A recent survey of the readers of *Company* magazine[2] found that more than half of the 5000 respondents believed that men who attacked women were 'usually socially or sexually inadequate', and nearly half felt such men were 'pathetic failures, who could only feel achievement by dominating others.'

In fact, in different types of rapist, different motives dominate.

Some *are* primarily sexually motivated. For others, sex is a means of creating fear or expressing anger, power, control or feelings of revenge, while a small group of men can only achieve arousal through violence.

# THE SEXUAL RAPIST

Sexual rapists are usually lacking in social and life skills and their normal manner is passive or submissive. They are loners who have low self-esteem. They find it difficult to start and maintain conversations, or to develop relationships with women. They may look inadequate; 'wimpish' is the derogatory term for it. They are often obsessed with their sexual inadequacy and feel the only way they can satisfy unusually strong sexual urges is by attack. Even so, their attacks should not be seen as an extension of their sexuality but of their tendency towards abusive behaviour.

Their approach to their victim is to make a sudden sexually explicit grab rather than start with a conversation or threats. But their fantasy is that their victims will respond to them by submitting willingly. Harry always hopes his victims will take a dominant role and actively enjoy sex with him. He says of his attacks on women: 'All I want is to be loved and cared for'.

Though sexual rapists start with the use of force, which can be very frightening, they do not relish violence for its own sake and will tend to use just enough force to make a woman submit. Of all men who sexually attack women, they are the most likely to back off if they meet verbal or physical resistance.

Such men usually have a history of petty sex offences – obscene phone calls, indecent exposure and minor sexual assault. They may ejaculate prematurely or have some other sexual dysfunction, another symptom of their sexual insecurity.

Ronald is a sexual rapist. As a schoolboy he was easily abused and bullied and was regarded as a wimp and an outsider. He was spotty and felt unattractive. He was unassertive and lacked any sense of purpose. His elder brother was an achiever and his younger sister was the focus of family attention. He had bed-wetting problems, felt rejected and in adolescence found it impossible to get girlfriends.

He first engaged in voyeurism by obsessively taking seats on buses that enabled him to look up women's dresses as they went upstairs. He would go into dress shops hoping to see women changing. After watching a television programme in which a man made obscene phone calls he began to make such calls and would try to persuade the recipients to undress. His first contact offence was frottage; he would rub up against women in under-ground trains. He progressed to indecent exposure and then to 'accidentally' touching women in swimming pools. He then began running up to women, putting his hand up their skirts and running off. He was a frightened and frightening young man on his way to becoming a rapist when he was first referred for counselling. He was masturbating five to seven times a day to fantasies of raping women.

# THE ANGER RAPIST

Anger rapists are usually men with a woman in their lives – a mother, girlfriend or wife – who they see as dominant and whom they fear and resent.

Their style may be macho. They may be attractive and have social graces but are insecure about their masculinity and become enraged if it is questioned. They regard women as demanding and tend to feel generally 'put down' and dominated by them. They either put them on a pedestal or see them as unfaithful or treacherous. They choose to blame women for their life problems.

Anger rapists gain release by exacting vengeance on unsus-pecting women. They act angrily. They may use weapons and unnecessary physical violence – strangling, punching, kicking. They may threaten mutilation or death, or harm to their victim's family. They are likely to commit sexual acts they regard as degrading of the victim – sodomy and oral sex. There have been cases of rapists urinating or defaecating on their victims. They daydream of situations where women cower from their advances. Their aim is to dominate, degrade and take their revenge.

Their attacks – usually on strangers – are often triggered by the breakdown of, or severe conflict within, an existing relationship, which makes them feel rejected. For this reason anger rapists are likely to attack within a few miles of their home. If the police knew they were looking for an anger rapist, the chances are they would not have to look far from the scene of the offence.

Anger rapists do not necessarily leap out at their victims from a hiding place. They may engage them in conversation in a pub or any public meeting place and then offer to escort them home or simply follow them, looking for an opportunity to grab them.

Mike's behaviour is typical of anger rapists. He is an extremely jealous and possessive man and is also prone to throwing childish tantrums. These qualities wreck the loving but over-dependent relationships he forms with women. As his partners inevitably struggle to assert some measure of freedom, he accuses them of unfaithfulness, insists on knowing everything about their movements and tries to restrict their outside interests and friendships. Because his behaviour is unreasonable, he cannot justify it except in terms of angry accusations against his partner. Inevitably he loses not only his quarrels with her but also her respect and affection.

Afraid of his own incredible anger with the person closest to him at each major defeat, he will storm out of the house shouting in his head: 'Bastard, bitch, bastard, bitch'. Upon his seeing other women, the refrain will change to, 'Bastards, bitches'. He feels extreme hatred for all women and will say to himself: 'Fuck them all. They won't put me down. Who do they think they are?' In this mood he will go through areas that he knows to be more deserted and might target a woman. His approach will be direct and extremely angry. He will say: 'You fucking bitch. Do as I say or I'm going to fucking kill you.' He may immediately use far more violence than is needed to gain control – getting his own back for what he sees as a collective rejection by the women in his life.

This example is so typical that some readers may think they recognise Mike. In fact, the name is chosen arbitrarily and the behaviour cycle described is a composite of the behaviour of several Mikes.

# THE SOCIO-PATHIC RAPIST

This is a fairly loose category of offenders who are primarily anti-social or criminal. They are into conquest sex and would resent being classified as sex offenders. They do not regard what they do as rape and justify their assaults by sentiments that pervade our culture – 'women ask for it', 'women who say no, don't mean no', 'for a woman to ask a man home is the same as agreeing to have sex' and 'women like being forced'.

Socio-pathic rapists may begin to rape women they come across while committing other crimes, particularly housebreaking, or may be found among those men who sexually harass women in the workplace. There is little to distinguish the actions of men who use the threat of physical force to gain a woman's sexual submission from those who use their powers to hire and fire, or promote and demote. Offenders may progress from this form of opportunism to deliberately picking up women with the intention of raping them. Such men attack in the homes of their victims or their own home. They are very selfish and calculating and experience rape primarily as just another form of anti-social behaviour.

However, the socio-pathic rapist shares the criminal's concern not to be caught. He uses minimal violence so as to leave no evidence. He generally relies on threats of violence to gain subjection. Though he may produce a weapon, he is unlikely to use it. He is likely to develop strategies that make conviction difficult.

Peter picks women up in discos and bars. He is intelligent, can be charming and appears to be perfectly normal. He rapes his victim in his or her home, or in his car. He threatens to strangle her if she does not obey him but says he never actually uses physical violence. If his victim refuses to be intimidated he will abandon his attack. By means of threats he makes his victim undress herself and him. He plays the lover, making the woman kiss and caress him before and after the rape. He generally uses a contraceptive. His intention is to undermine his victim's claim and her confidence in her claim to having been raped at all.

If a prosecution ensues, the kind of questioning she can expect from the defence barrister might be as follows:

'Did you take your own clothes off? Answer yes or no.'

'Did you take his clothes off. Answer yes or no.'

'Did he use a contraceptive? Answer yes or no. A strange thing for a rapist to do.'

'Did you give him a kiss after the so-called rape?'

But with no signs of violence and no weapons used, this type of case is unlikely to reach the courts in the first place.

One socio-pathic rapist was questioned by police several times for alleged rapes of holidaymakers. Twice the police had too little evidence to charge him, once he was charged but there was too little evidence to commit him to Crown Court and once he was acquitted. He was finally convicted only after he came under investigation into an allegation of rape while he was on bail for yet another rape. The socio-pathic rapist is the most difficult to distinguish as well as convict. There are many variations.

Julian can be a charming person when everything is going his way but becomes belligerent when they do not. He believes he is God's gift to women. He boasts about his ability to 'pull the birds'. When he has a 'girlfriend', he takes her to places he wants to go, whether she wants to or not – often to places he can display her to his mates. In male company, he will ignore her and brush aside any protest at his treatment of her. Whether his behaviour has angered her or not he will still insist on sex when they are alone. The more she objects the more insistent he becomes, until through a blend of bullying, persistence and exercise of brute strength he gets his way. He does not think of this as rape.

Dave rapes within the context of a permanent relationship, though neither he nor his partner would acknowledge that what takes place is rape. His common-law wife complains that he frequently uses physical violence on her after drinking bouts and also forces her to have sex against her will, reflecting an attitude that she is his property. While she feels her complaints of being battered are justified, she accepts his sexual abuse of her as the social norm. She is afraid to leave because of his violence and because she is economically dependent on him.

# THE SADISTIC RAPIST

Thankfully, sadistic rapists are rare because they are also the most dangerous and deranged among men who attack women. Their victim's fear, pain and perhaps death is their main turn-on and they may go to extreme lengths to indulge it. They may take or lure their victims to a safe place where they can be sure of keeping them for several hours without fear of being disturbed. Their manner will not be angry but cold. They may use implements in their sexual attack and may bite or otherwise torture or mutilate their victims. They may develop into the type of 'serial' rapist or rapist-killer who terrorises a whole neighbour-hood. Some such attackers develop bizarre 'trademarks', such as particular ways of physically marking their victims. There are different types.

Some will be extravert and possibly aggressive in social situations, will dress loudly, express the idea that women like being knocked about. They may have inflicted pain on partners in 'normal' sexual relationships before moving on to rape. One man said he enjoyed pulling out the pubic hairs of his partners while 'making love'. He maintained that most women he had sex with had enjoyed a degree of violence.

Others are over-controlled and obsessive, likely to be conservative and fastidious in manner and appearance and may have a strong religious background. They may regard themselves as punishing their victims for having seduced them to 'sin'. This kind of sexual attacker may ritualistically cleanse himself by symbolically mutilating the body of the women he has raped and killed.

The masturbatory fantasy of one sadistic rapist is of a young woman being raped by someone else. She is in a state of terror and her attacker begins strangling her. He rescues her by stabbing and killing her assailant. He comforts the woman and she is filled with gratitude. Then, gradually, he begins to strangle and rape her himself.

Sadists are the least likely to be diverted by any ploy the victim might attempt. Though a violent reaction from the victim might only further provoke their fury, it may also, if the opportunity presented itself, be the only hope she would have of escape.

If typologies were to be relied on and human beings were governed solely by logic, it should be possible to conceive of a phased response to rape attack which would eliminate the most easily deterred type of assailant without risking provoking the most dangerous to greater excesses.

And there do seem to be some simple lessons to be drawn from the knowledge that rapists are not all of a kind. For instance, the knowledge that sexual rapists may be repelled by a clear verbal rebuff means that that should be a good first response to any kind of sexual attack. It might just bring an end to the ordeal then and there.

# THE RAPE PROCESS

Rape is essentially an attempt by a person or group to subject another individual to their control. It is not a single event but a process made up of several phases. Each phase theoretically offers opportunity for the victim to retain and exercise a measure of control, however limited, and so restrict the experience of being overpowered.

What is suggested is not a fixed plan of action; not all the phases may occur in any one attack or be so well defined. The phases described here are based on rapists' accounts of how they behave and have been affected by their victim's response.

# PHASE ONE —
# PLANNING THE ATTACK

Sexual attacks seem spontaneous but most have been planned at least in some respects and rely partly on the victims' lack of caution and preparedness.

Even before an attack is consciously planned, in many cases it is slowly formulated in the flawed sexual imagination of the assailant.

Men, like women, masturbate to fantasies. While 'normal' masturbatory fantasies of both sexes occasionally include elements of force, the fantasies indulged in by sex offenders may consistently focus on attacks on women. Such fantasies are refined over a period of time – sometimes over months or years – and reinforced each time the fantasiser ejaculates. With men with high sex drives, that could happen several times a day. It seems a reasonable deduction that the more an individual's masturbatory fantasies deviate from what is generally accepted as normal, the greater difficulty he will have translating the fantasy into real experience with the voluntary co-operation of a partner.

According to some experts, not all rapists fantasise about rape. But, in the author's experience, the majority of sex offenders of all types masturbate at least sometimes to images of rapes they have committed.

In terms of his masturbatory fantasy, an offender can be likened to an obsessive dramatist/director who casts and recasts himself in the lead role. When he tries to translate his 'drama' to the stage of the real world he uses force to make some hapless woman play the role he has invented. His action is not against her as an individual. He has no sense of her real identity, and very little or no sense of the full impact on her of his actions. He is acting out something he has played out in his head many times. In one case, a man who raped a mother and daughter had written out his fantasy of the attack in full prior to the rape. The police came across the document on searching the man's home. They also found sadistic pornography and his own attempt to write sadistic pornography in which his own wife was cast in the role of victim.

An important part of the treatment of offenders is to awaken in them an awareness of how their actions *have* affected their victims. For some it is like waking from a dream. They break into tears when they finally acknowledge the pain and damage they have caused, though whether the sorrow they display is for themselves or their victim is debatable.

One way a victim may hope to alter the course of the drama the rapist has scripted and rehearsed – both in other rapes he has committed and in his fantasies – is to convince him she is not the creature of his imagination and is inappropriate for the role.

An unusual example of this is given by a woman who worked as a prostitute.[9] She tells of a man who stopped his car in a city street, ostensibly to help her, when the strap of one of her shoes had broken. Failing to mend the shoe, he offered her a lift to her home. Instead he drove her out of town to an isolated spot, produced a gun and ordered her to undress. She laughed as she began to take her clothes off and said: 'If it was sex you wanted why didn't you say so? I'm a prostitute. You didn't need to waste all this money on petrol. We could have gone straight to my place.' The man surprised her by leaning over the steering wheel and breaking into tears. He ordered her to get dressed and get out of the car and then drove off leaving her by the roadside. Her reaction, clearly a survival technique, and the man's response illustrate that rape is not about sex.

Perhaps sexual rapists are easily deterred by verbal confrontation because ready acquiescence to their attack by the victim is an important part of their fantasy. The fantasy requires the victim's compliance. Sexual rapists proceed with attacks on women who offer them little or no opposition. They don't consider that the victim might be too paralysed by fear to protest. They accept acquiescence as confirmation of their fantasy – that the woman was impressed by their commanding approach and wanted to be raped. Conversely, with the sadistic rapist, his victim's terror, possibly expressed in a desperate struggle, only confirms her in the role already scripted for her.

Apart from the detailed preparation for an attack in fantasy and any practical planning he may have done, the attacker often has the benefit of previous experience.

Rapists will seek out areas where there is least chance of interruption to which to take their victims or where women sometimes go alone. Anger rapists, for example, will tend to know of isolated places in the areas where they operate. Some will have worked out escape routes. Rapists favour not only deserted and darkened streets and lanes, but such places as multi-storey car parks or shopping centres after business hours. Some men follow habitual routines, taking the opportunity to rape as it arises. A man who raped women on trains would travel for many weeks late at night waiting to get a woman alone in a carriage. Another followed women home at night hoping they would go past an isolated spot. Sometimes he would follow a couple of women to see if they would go different ways.

The date-and-acquaintance rapist will usually attack in his victim's or his own home, in a car, or at a common meeting place – a school or counselling office, at unusual hours. One teacher would rape children in deserted classrooms during the lunch break. An American study shows that, of 100 rapes over a particular period, 35 were committed between 7pm and midnight, 40 between midnight and 7am and 20 between midday and 7pm. Almost half of them took place in the victims' homes and 15 in cars.[10]

A rapist will often target a particular type of woman, possibly one who looks vulnerable, and will let others pass. In a recent television interview one offender said he never went for pretty women – he was too afraid of their disdain. Similarly others will not go for confident-looking women. But yet others make a point of attacking pretty or confident women.

Women understandably resent the fact that while rape is basically a man's problem, it is they who must take special precautions. But there is no doubt that by taking some practical measures women can reduce the chances of becoming rape victims.

Some that are commonly recommended and worth heeding are:

• Get to know the area you live in.
• Ask yourself on any specific occasion whether you really need to go into an isolated and badly-lit area unaccompanied.

- Take simple security measures in your home. Fit door chains and peep-holes, participate in community watch programmes and do not heed any embarrassment you may feel about denying someone access, even if you know them.
- Ask for proof of identification of people who say they are from gas or electricity companies or the police.
- Approach your front door key in hand, to reduce the chances of being caught fumbling in your own doorway and bundled into your home by an assailant.
- Do not accept lifts, or invite home or go to the home of a man you feel at all unsure about.
- Avoid hitch-hiking or using the services of unorthodox taxi operators.

# PHASE TWO — THE APPROACH

Although different types of sexual attacker may announce themselves by differences of approach or manner – a sexual rapist by making a sudden sexual grab, an anger rapist displaying anger – these are no more than indicators. In judging whether people are well- or ill-disposed to us we all have to rely on our intuition.

Through intuition, we respond to cues that we may not be consciously aware of. Particularly where it comes to danger, our intuitive response is to be trusted, if only because generally speaking there is not much harm done if we are wrong.

Because women are socialised to be helpful and polite and to put the feelings of others, particularly of men, before their own, they may be tolerant when they should be rude or linger when they should run. A rapist will take the fullest advantage of any indecisiveness in his victim's response towards him.

Offenders often make several unsuccessful approaches to women before they manage to rape one. Rapists who have killed women have told how, on the day of a killing, they approached other women who made some gesture (perhaps of impatience or suggesting they would draw attention to themselves), or dismissed them rudely, or simply refused to engage in discussion with them and so avoided becoming the victim. One woman targeted by a rapist simply looked at her watch as though waiting for a friend. That was enough to make him abandon her as a target. Another woman he followed knocked on the door of a nearby house. He didn't wait to see if she was known there.

Before he went on to kill Shirley Banks of Bristol, John Cannan threatened a woman in a car. He pointed a gun at her – she slammed the door on his hand and drove off at high speed.

Some women appear to be too embarrassed or afraid to demand help from strangers when they are threatened or feel threatened. However, rapists are deterred by any action of their victims likely to draw other people's attention. Pretending to greet another person as though they were known to you and asking them to accompany you for a while would be enough to deflect many assailants. Sad to say, there are always easier targets to be found.

Some women display extraordinary levels of trust in, or reluctance to offend, strangers or people whom they hardly know. A serial rapist and killer in America would present himself as a photographer for a true detective magazine. He persuaded women to model for him in their underclothes and went on taking pictures while he killed them.

Whereas some attackers will stop pursuing a woman who moves decisively away from an approach, a gradual speeding up is likely only to excite them. They feel they are already beginning to frighten and control the person they have targeted.

If you feel any misgivings about an approach – even one that is ostensibly flatterng or asking for help – break into a determined run towards a more populated or built-up area. Don't worry about giving offence. The more determined you are to get away, the more precipitative and openly violent and therefore attention-attracting must be the attacker's effort if he is to restrain you. Kick off your shoes if they slow you down and discard any other impediments such as shopping or a handbag.

If you are still pursued, you should continue running and

might try shouting 'Fire' rather than 'Help' – it is likely to surprise the attacker and people may respond to you more readily if they do not anticipate violence. You should do anything likely to draw attention to yourself and not fret about what people might think or the possibility that you are making a mistake. It is better to be wrong than go through an experience likely to endanger your life and leave you with long-term psychological and possibly physical scars.

# PHASE THREE –
# ONSET OF THE ATTACK

The victim will be subjected to varying degrees of violence, or threatened with dire consequences if she does not do as she is told.

Rapists often find, and come to expect, that the violence of their approach will leave their victims in a state of shock. Women who at this stage can manage to convey that they are not vulnerable, stunned individuals fumbling for a response are very disconcerting. Their reaction means that the script the rapist has in his head is already beginning to let him down. The sexual or socio-pathic rapist may abandon his attack if he senses that his victim is not easily defeated and likely to be more trouble than she's worth.

But deterring the rapist is not necessarily the most immediate advantage a woman can seek to gain – at the most basic level she may try to put her assailant off-guard sufficiently for her to take some physical action or attempt to escape. She may just play for time, increasing the chance of outside intervention. The study mentioned above[10] showed that, in the period in which 100 rapes were committed, there were another 145 rapes attempted. Interruption is the most common single reason rapists abandon attacks. At a deeper level of subtlety, a woman may, through a varied and flexible response, hope to build up psychological power over her attacker.

A problem for the victim is that she cannot be sure what type of attacker she is dealing with. Whether real or bluff, the threats will sound convincing and may be backed up either by indications of violence (hands round the throat, or the showing of a weapon) or varying degrees of actual violence. The way threats are phrased can give clues to the seriousness of intention behind them – 'I'll hurt you if you don't do as I say' is more aggressive than, 'Do as I say and I won't hurt you'. Someone who used the latter phraseology might be more easily deterred than someone using the former.

Obviously if threats are delivered with convincing levels of violence they are likely to be real. Whatever the intentions of the rapist, his verbal threats may be extremely crude. Because there are rapists who are capable of carrying out such threats, immediate defiance of a specific threat is not advisable, unless the victim feels particularly confident she has the upper hand psychologically.

However, the command 'Be quiet' does not mean 'Don't struggle' and it does not mean the victim should not attempt to communicate again after a lapse of time. 'Don't move' does not mean 'Don't try to talk your way out of the situation'. The problem for people who assume control over others is how to phrase commands that produce the results they want. Rape is as much a psychological as a physical struggle, with the attacker attempting to frighten his victim into subjection. Exercising rationality by a limited literal response to commands is one way the victim can assert herself and hope to retain an element of control without directly challenging her attacker in a way that might provoke more violence. While being verbally assertive, the rape survivor should avoid any temptation to put down or ridicule her assailant.

# PHASE FOUR —
# PERSON TO PERSON

If verbal assertiveness fails, the victim may still hope to get through to her assailant, first by appeals for sympathy for herself and then by attempts at establishing empathy with her attacker.

Sympathy may succeed, particularly where such appeals suggest the victim as being an inappropriate sex object. Some attackers have been put off by victims who have told them, truthfully or otherwise, they are having their period, are pregnant and afraid for the unborn child, are suffering from gynaecological infections, venereal disease and even mental illness or bereavement. Most of the rapists in counselling sessions with the author have felt this kind of approach would be the most likely to put them off. None has said he would be put off by a victim who said she was a virgin and wanted to remain one, though this appeal has been known to work. And by no means all men are put off by menstruation.

One man told of a woman he had attacked who had said she had cancer of the womb and had just learned it was untreatable. This led to a long conversation which ended when he said she could go if she promised not to tell anyone. She made the promise and he let her go.

Establishing empathy requires a more positive approach. It may help reduce the level of fear in the person doing the empathising and it offers the assailant the possibility of an unhumiliating withdrawal from the process he has started.

Empathy features in hostage and abduction training. Potential victims are taught to build a relationship rapidly with their abductor or hijacker. Some rapists, like hijackers and professional torturers, also recognise the 'danger' of allowing such a relationship to develop and cover their victims' heads or hide their own faces behind masks or dark glasses to reduce the possibility.

The extreme violence some rapists employ from the outset

may also be partly designed to minimise the possibility of any relationship developing with their victims except that of domination and subjection. Some rapists give their victims no chance to start a conversation, though if such a man intends to rape a woman more than once, the lull after the first attack may afford an opportunity. Men commonly experience a post-ejaculatory mood change, which may take the form of an emotional low. It has been suggested that if they are doing something they regard as 'wrong' (adulterous sex as much as rape), it is at this point that they will be vulnerable to feelings of guilt.

Advice given to potential hostages might be helpful. The victim could try to make it clear to the assailant that she is not the woman he has in mind nor an appropriate sex object. She could give him her first name and personalise herself. 'My name is Judith. What is your name? I've read about this sort of thing. I don't know why people have to be so horrible to each other, do you?' One can help build a sense of rapport with another person by slowing down one's breathing and speaking in more measured and softer tones.[11] One offender spoke of an attack in which the woman had looked into his face with tears in her eyes. It was a look not of fear but sorrow. She had gently squeezed his arm as she talked to him as if trying to understand. It took him back to an occasion when, as a child, he had been incredibly angry and his aunt had acted in a very similar way. He became confused and ran off. Another rapist said: 'In a strange way I never saw the victim. I just felt an incredible rage towards my mother. At one stage I thought it was my mother.'

Some rapists will respond favourably to sympathetic questioning – about themselves and why they feel the need to attack women, about the problems they must be facing to behave as they do, problems about women, bad past experiences.

The following is the kind of cycle the victim may be trying to disengage herself from. John (an anger rapist) has attacked women with varying degrees of severity since the age of 12. He describes how it feels for him: 'Before I attack I am usually depressed, tired, feeling unwanted and quick-tempered. I could have money troubles. I will have had an argument. I feel rejected. To escape all this I decide to take it out on a woman. When I have had my way sexually – whether it be rape or exposure – I feel more relaxed and in control of myself.'

Rapists may be susceptible to talk about their feelings of rejection and loneliness, their frustration at having again been unable to control their behaviour. The longer a rapist lets his victim talk, the more likely she is to succeed in talking him out of his aggression and ending the attack. Even if she does not avoid rape, she may well reduce the degree of violence used against her. Probably one of the few clear rules about response to a rape attack is that the victim should stop talking with her assailant only if ordered directly to do so or when she feels out of danger. When the talking ends, the rapist will either proceed with his attack or withdraw.

An attempt at empathy needs to be convincing. If the rapist feels he is being manipulated or losing control or simply being delayed in the hope of someone coming to the rescue, or lulled into a false sense of security which might give his victim a chance to run for it, he may suddenly reassert himself.

If at any time an assailant tells his victim to go, or leaves her with the opportunity to escape, she should promptly take it. Such a man is quite likely to change his mind or go through another mood swing. Several rapists have told of occasions when they have left their victims unattended, almost as though they were giving them a chance to escape. Women have been left in rooms, cars and even outside buildings while the rapist went away, sometimes after merely ordering them to stay put. Almost invariably in such accounts the woman does wait – presumably too afraid to move – in some cases only to be raped again.

# PHASE FIVE – THE ATTACK

The attacker will employ threats and varying degrees of violence to get his victim to do what he wants. Even where the victim is physically overpowered she may not be defeated psychologically. The man may set out to annihilate her sense of self-worth. He may call her a whore or a slut, or a bitch, or shit. But it is possible for an assailant to say and do degrading things to a person without succeeding in making them feel degraded.

It might be helpful for a victim to remind herself that the attack is not being made upon her as an individual. She has been arbitrarily selected as a member of her sex and possibly because, for very subjective reasons, the rapist sees her as belonging to a particular type. A victim, and particularly one with a poor self-image, may experience rape as evidence that she is someone not deserving of love, kindness or respect. The conclusion is, 'If this person can treat me like this perhaps I am really like this.' But she is not experiencing a judgement so much as an attitude towards women that is prevalent in society finding ultimate expression in the actions of the rapist, who is delivering to her the accumulated distillation of his own distorted thinking and embittered life experience.

The amount of resistance a woman offers will be determined by what she feels about the invasion of her body, the degree of violence used on her and the extent to which she is disabled by fear. It may be helpful to consider three levels of physical resistance.

The first level would not be seen as a direct physical challenge by the attacker – more of a human response to a life-threatening situation – and may well act as a deterrent. It would include such things as urinating, fainting and throwing epileptic-type fits.

The next stage would be putting up a struggle to protect oneself – becoming awkward. The main value of this is playing for time. Struggling may also excite some attackers and even cause ejaculation before penetration takes place. Some women have also managed to avoid penetration by taking an active role sexually once it has become clear rape is inevitable. Such action avoids the risk of venereal disease and pregnancy and may reduce the amount of violence a woman is subjected to but it may also make it more difficult to get her attacker convicted.

The third level of physical resistance is attack. If a woman is prepared to increase the risk to her life to avoid rape, she will attack. It should be attempted when the rapist is most vulnerable and only to gain an opportunity for escape.

Gang rapes are worth some special attention, particularly as they appear to be on the increase and can be singularly horrific. Most of the men in the author's experience who have been involved in gang rape have been of the socio-pathic type and involved in teenage attacks on teenage girls. Some have described themselves as having been carried along by the power of the group and under great pressure to conform. Members of such groups who are reluctant to take part are often taunted and ridiculed or threatened. In some attacks, boyfriends are abducted or waylaid along with the rape victim and are made to watch.

Gang rapes offer the victim little opportunity for establishing any meaningful dialogue with her assailants as they take place in an atmosphere of boisterous macho 'humour' and derision. Offenders assert that women take such humour in good part and that gang rapes are not so bad because the victim does not have to fear being killed. This glossing over of the terrible impact of such an attack on the rape survivor is typical of offender rationalisations.

The victim's only hope of the attack being prematurely ended without outside intervention is if there is a reluctant member of the gang whose feelings she might play on in the hope of winning him over to her side.

For whatever reasons, some women manage to stay mentally in control to a remarkable degree even when they are being raped. Harry broke into a woman's bedroom and placed a bag over her head. He threatened her and ran the blade of a knife up and down her back while he raped her. Though terrified, she deliberately felt his body for distinguishing marks. She mentally noted the texture of his hair, whether he had a moustache or beard, the things he did to her and the sound of his voice so she would be able to give the police as much information as possible. It was a way of asserting herself even while she had minimal control. Under careful and sympathetic questioning, she was able to give three full pages of description of an attacker she had never seen. Her detailed description led directly to Harry's arrest. This was in the United States where the police in some states use a process known as psychological profiling, the techniques of which have now been partly adopted in the UK.

By systematically gathering information likely to help secure the arrest of her attacker, the victim of rape can retain some sense of control even when she is physically overpowered.

Most of the time we take in impressions of other people without any conscious effort. Preparing oneself to describe someone is a job of work. Some of the things the rape victim can try to remember at the time of the rape that will assist in the identification and successful prosecution of a rapist are:

1  *The approach* Were there any suspicious events before the attack? How does the rapist approach his victim? Is he subtle, seductive, aggressive, cunning, or does he make a surprise attack? What words does he use?

2  *Intimidation* Does he use threats? What kind of threats? Does he reinforce his threats with physical force or weapons (rope or other material)? What words does he use; any unusual phrases? Does he have a weapon? What sort? How does he use the weapon? Does he relinquish the weapon at any time? What level of force is used?

3  *Control and interaction* Does he continue to use threats or violence to control? If so, how? Does he use ridicule? What rewards, if any, does he promise? What is his manner (boasting, apologetic)? Does he give the impression of having executed such an attack before? Is he worried about being identified or injured? Does he betray knowledge of police procedure?

4  *Sexual activities* Does he make demands about clothing or make other specific requests? What does he do without making a request or demand? Does he enforce vaginal, oral, anal or varied sex? Does he insist on kissing? What does he say and in what kind of terminology? Does the attack involve gross indecency? What does he force his victim to say and do? How does he react if a demand is denied? Is there any dysfunction,

such as premature or retarded ejaculation? Is there a demand to wear certain clothing, an interest in items of clothing or a part of the body (for instance, feet)? What is the sequence of his sexual behaviour?

5 *Verbal expression* What does he say during the attack? Precisely what words does he use? How would his accent and tone of voice best be described? Does he undergo changes in mood or attitude? How does he leave his victim – making threats, or apologising? Does he take anything?

6 *Physical characteristics to note* Colour and texture of hair, shape of nose, ears, eyes, jaw. Any scars, tattoos, moles? Does he have a moustache, beard – if so, what sort? Is he circumcised? What clothing and shoes does he wear? Does he try to disguise himself?

The woman who tries to gather information of this kind about her attacker should be careful to give no impression to the rapist that she is doing so.

# PHASE SIX – AFTER THE RAPE

Though the rape has taken place, this is the most critical phase – the victim is probably the only person with evidence that could send the attacker to prison. If reported cases are anything to go by, it is fairly rare for rapists to kill their victims. But the introduction of longer sentences for rape means that such assailants may now serve similar sentences whether they kill or not.

Rapists have various ways of leaving their victims. A man who is confident he cannot be identified may simply leave his victim or, for instance, dump her out of a car.

Another may threaten to harm her or her children if she reports the attack. He may apologise and ask his victim to promise not to inform on him. Either way, he is looking for assurances that his victim will not report him.

Statements that have reassured rapists have been that the

victim is far too ashamed to tell anyone, is afraid of her husband or boyfriend finding out, does not want to bring shame on her family, thinks that nobody will believe her anyway.

The moment the attacker offers to let the victim go, she should do so. As already noted, rapists may go through marked changes of mood.

Once free, the survivor of a rape attack has to decide whether to report it or not. It is well established that women who keep totally silent and bottle their experience up inside themselves suffer psychologically for many years, if not the rest of their lives. Some of the psychological consequences of rape are loss of pleasure in sex, an enduring sense of guilt, fear of men, anxiety, loss of ambition, withdrawal from the world. A particularly cruel legacy of rape and the sexual abuse of children can be the infiltration of the woman's own sexuality by the rape experience. Intrusive thoughts of rape experienced by most survivors are a reliving of the trauma. But a few women, particularly those abused in childhood, may begin to find fantasies of rape sexually stimulating. This can strengthen their feeling of guilt, whereas it should always be seen as another damaging legacy of the rape.

The reasons why women do not report rape are complex. One is fear of involvement in the legal processes – unsympathetic and even disparaging questioning in the courts and lack of sensitivity by the police. Going through the legal process has been described by some as worse than the rape itself and it can directly reinforce the experience of worthlessness transmitted through rape. Julie, now an in-patient in a psychiatric hospital, has begun only in her mid-thirties to work with her hospital social worker on what was probably the main cause of her psychiatric illness. As a 15-year-old she accepted a lift at night. The driver sadistically raped her. She found her way to a house whose occupants telephoned the police, her parents and a doctor. On arriving at the house, the distraught father slapped her face and rebuked her for hitching a lift. The doctor prescribed tranquillisers which blocked out the trauma and he told the police that she was too disturbed to be able to give evidence. The police reassured her that the man would try to rape again and they would catch him. The man did rape again and Julie blamed herself for not having prevented the rape by giving evidence.

There have been some improvements in the police processing of rape cases. In some areas survivors are now interviewed in special interview rooms and by police women. But the system still falls far short of what is desirable. Procedures can change fairly quickly but underlying attitudes – for instance those concerning women's culpability for rape – are slow to change. However, the police have begun to see the need for special training in the handling of rape cases and there are now a variety of courses available.

There are important arguments for going to the police. Gail Abarbanel at the Santa Monica Rape Treatment Centre in California argues that to discourage women from reporting is 'a bad message that implies the victim has a role in the rape'.

From a crime prevention perspective, it is relevant that men who rape are likely to go on raping and are encouraged to do so each time they get away with it.

If all sexual offences – including the so-called 'milder' offences of indecent phone calls and indecent assault – were reported, it would expose the extent of the problem and provide a flow of information that could lead to the more effective identification of offenders.

However, any rape survivor who chooses not to report should not hold herself responsible for contributing to subsequent attacks. The rapist is responsible for every attack and its consequences. Furthermore, the police, the law fraternity and society at large perpetuate attitudes which contribute to the decision of so many rape survivors to keep their ordeal to themselves.

Rape Crisis has developed great expertise in helping rape victims survive their ordeal. They do not pressurise people who consult them to go to the police but give them every support if they decide to do so. By talking to them and to close friends or relatives, victims of rape can be helped to overcome the legacy of fear, self-blame, loss of self-respect and rage they are often left with. Telephone numbers for local Rape Crisis groups can be found in the phone book.

# THE RAPE AND SEXUAL ASSAULT OF CHILDREN

The rape and assault of children is possibly more common than that of women.[12] N Cager and S Schuur in *Sexual Assault: Confronting Rape in America* suggest that there are more than a million child victims a year in the US. They wrote: 'Little girls, like their mothers before them, learn at an early age to endure being sexually used. A few experiences of the disbelief, shock, shame, embarrassment and anger of those closest to them provides good training in silence.'

Often children who do report incidents find they are not believed or even worse are held to be partly to blame. Even if there is some recognition of what the child has gone through, people find it difficult to face up to the trauma and damage such experiences cause. This tendency to minimise their importance or attempt to limit the damage by suppressing the experience leaves the victims to 'bear the secret pain alone'. Only much later in life do some women find themselves able to confide to another person that they were abused in childhood.

Julie was 30 years old when, during a counselling session, she first told of how her stepfather had tied her to her bed as a child and raped her.

Mary was 28 before she could speak of having been raped in the back of a cab in her early teens by a taxi-driver.

Sandra was forced to have sex with her father throughout her childhood. She was 50 before she was able to talk of it.

Michelle was picked up by a sadistic rapist at the age of 12. She was taken to a forest where she was beaten, threatened with a knife and raped. Despite her injuries she could not bring herself to tell her parents or anyone else in authority. She said she had fallen off her bike. She feels her parents did not believe her but also did not want to know more. She was in her forties before she told another person of the attack.

Probably many more women find they can never talk about abuse suffered in childhood. The accounts of both offenders and the survivors of sexual abuse suggest that it is far more common than the reported cases suggest.

Roger experienced his daughter trying to tell of his abuse of her on four occasions. She tried to tell her mother who simply informed him that she was telling fibs about him. He smacked her by way of punishment. She tried to tell NSPCC officials but, after interviewing him, they took no action. She told her relatives and her teachers. The fact that she had told several people was successfully represented by him as evidence that it was all her fantasy. He continued to abuse her, and his daughter now says that she sees herself as having been abused by the system as much as by her own father.

As with men who commit sexual offences against women, paedophiles often own up in counselling sessions and treatment programmes to many more offences than they have been prosecuted for. One, a former child counsellor, confessed on a Thames Television *TV Eye* programme to having offended more than 2000 times.[13]

It is common for parents to warn their children to be wary of approaches by adults they do not know – 'Don't take sweets from strangers' is the well-worn injunction. In the past ten years we have learned that it is probably much more important to find ways to protect children from adults they do know. Eighty per cent of recorded cases of sexual abuse of children in the UK between 1983 and 1987 took place in the children's own homes.[14]

Despite the extensive media coverage given to child sexual abuse in recent years, the cases that still tend to attract most news interest are the more sensational – those involving the abduction or murder of children.

Some men who sexually attack children are sadists. One described how he deliberately raped his child victims on rough concrete or gravel floors to increase the pain he inflicted. There are a number of magazines and newsletters circulated to paedophiles, some of them internationally. An article in one invites readers to consider the pleasures of the brutal rape of young children. Even where an attacker is not sadistic, physical damage can be an inevitable consequence of sex between an adult and a child. Children as young as one year have been the victims of rape.

Adults who sexually abuse children have been categorised as fixated or regressed paedophiles.[15]

The fixated paedophile is not usually sexually aroused by adults, may only be really comfortable in the company of children and have no enduring relationships with people of his own age. What friends he has are likely to be other paedophiles. Many men in this category have been sexually abused as children and have incorporated their experiences of abuse into their own sexuality. They may prefer boys to girls. Many have a problem with sexual maturity; the appearance of body hair may disqualify children from their interest.

The regressed paedophile is someone who may have a stable relationship with a woman or be sexually attracted to women, though he may also be insecure about his sexuality and be immature in his relationship with them.

He is said to be likely to molest a child impulsively after or during a crisis. He may have a drink problem, or have lost his job, or be suffering from depression. He may 'pseudo-mature' the child – treating and thinking about him or her as an adult – or regress, seeking comfort and support from the child. His offence leaves him feeling deeply shamed though it will not stop him offending again next time he experiences personal difficulties.

The author finds it useful to distinguish some additional categories, among them the inadequate paedophile and the inadequate fixated paedophile. The former may be suffering from a mental handicap, senility or mental illness and be mentally immature. He has a problem with sexuality because he finds it difficult to form relationships. He may be seen as a social misfit. He is insecure and his sexual behaviour is motivated largely by curiosity. He sees children as non-threatening.

The inadequate fixated paedophile lacks interpersonal skills to develop relationships with children. He molests very young children or children he hasn't met before. He may offer children small sums of money for sex. He fits the caricature of the dirty old man who hangs around schools and public lavatories. He may expose himself or make obscene phone calls to children and will use child prostitutes. He is lonely and isolated and usually an older person.

The regressed category may, in fact, be less useful than we imagine, having more to do with the way paedophile behaviour is interpreted than any intrinsic difference. There is a tendency in court reports, and among paedophiles themselves, to excuse their offences in terms of one-off reactions to stress or some sort of breakdown in the family.

In a recent incest appeal case, where the sentence was increased for the first time from three to six years, Lord Lane announced guidance for future sentencing. Mitigating circumstances identified in incest cases were based on traditional sexual abuse myths. They included the promiscuity or seductiveness of the child. The age of a child was seen as relevant to whether a father should be imprisoned. In fact, no daughter of 16 is likely to develop a sexual relationship with her father. Wherever a father is found to be having sex with a daughter in the latter part of her teens, he has almost certainly been abusing her for years. It seems little has changed from the days of the drafting of the Leviticus laws of the Old Testament which admonish sons and daughters not to have sex with their mothers and fathers, rather than the other way round.

Paedophiles explain and excuse their actions to themselves and to counsellors in a variety of ways. David raped his step-daughter 'to punish her' for not accepting him in the home, not showing him enough affection and for rejecting him and 'putting him down' in front of his wife. Brian says that he became sexually involved with his daughter through administering 'punishment'. Even at 15 she was still being smacked by him on her bared behind. If she rebelled, he instead subjected her to sexual abuse.

Others claim that it was the child who seduced them, an argument that has also sometimes found support in the courts. One man recently told a court that his toddler stepson had kept putting his bare bottom provocatively near his penis. Another in a counselling session said he had fallen asleep with his step-daughter on his lap and awoke to find her hand in his flies. It was she who had taken the initiative. Asked what he'd have done if he'd found her with her hand in his wallet, he responded promptly: 'I'd have told her to leave it alone'.

Some men justify their actions by rationalising that it is good for a child to learn about sex in the safety of the home or that it is better for a man to have sex with a child to keep a marriage together than go outside the family to have an affair.

Many will blame their wife's sexual inadequacy, another argu-ment that has been upheld in court judgements. One father who abused his own child, asked in a treatment programme who was responsible, replied that 75 per cent of the responsibility was his wife's, because she was uninterested sexually, put him down and failed to encourage him in his work. His daughter was 'five per cent responsible' because she never refused his attentions and was always available. He accepted 20 per cent of the blame but in explaining that 20 per cent, he blamed his wife twice for making him angry.

Many offenders simply say that both they and the children enjoy the sex and they may argue that other cultures accept sex between adults and children. Paedophiles also claim that they are caring towards children who are otherwise neglected. The sex is not damaging and a small price to pay for the child to have an experience of being cared for.

Beneath the veneer of such excuses, offenders are responding to a range of motivations: an impulse to exercise power abusively over the powerless, fear of the world of adults and an inability to form close relationships with adults, a misplaced desire to take revenge against women in general by damaging the symbol of their love and affection, and a view of women and children as the property of males.[16] Many men are reproducing their own abusive childhood sexual experience.

The abduction and rape as opposed to the more common seduction of children is more likely to be anger-motivated. One sex offender who stabbed a little girl many times after his release from prison said: 'If I can't have my daughter, they can't have theirs'.

Paedophiles can be extremely skilled at gaining access to children. Few parents, trying to warn against abduction by strangers, will anticipate the variety of approaches or of personalities. The sadistic sexual attacker of children may be intelligent, socially skilled and have a good opinion of himself. His attacks on children will be triggered by some incident in his own life. There are men who have pretended to be, and even dressed up as, policemen or ministers of religion. One who did so told a child he had targeted: 'Your mother has had an accident. You must come quickly'. Another told a child at the end of school: 'Your mummy has asked me to pick you up'. Some men use threats or offer money to get children to comply with their wishes.

Paedophiles who generally rely on seduction are sexually orientated towards children. They are expert at identifying vulnerable children – they tend to target those who are insecure and lonely or neglected. They seduce them over a period of time with a blend of flattery, affection and bribes. They know how to talk to children, or more especially they know how to listen and assume a paternal role. They will find out what is troubling a child at school and at home and develop the role of a trusted counsellor. They will become to the children what the parents have failed to become and will subtly turn a social relationship into a sexual one, starting with ambiguous touching and withdrawing if the reaction is bad, only to try again later. Seduction of a child can take place over months and even years. This manipulation of the child is not necessarily pursued at a conscious level. Paedophiles rationalise their behaviour in the same way as do the rest of us.

If necessary, they will cultivate the parents so as to disarm them of fears they might have for their child and to give their relationship with the child the semblance of parental endorsement. A common reaction by members of a community to exposure of a paedophile is, 'I would never have believed it. He really liked kids'.

Robert has been moved out of his home for sexually abusing his daughter. But he also abused other children in his street without being detected.

While decorating the outside of his home, he would ask children if they could help by holding the ladder, for example. He would eventually ask them in for a drink. He would give them a few pence. He would invite them to play on the computer. He would ask the children to be sure to tell their parents where they were and would check up, saying: 'Do your parents know you are here? If not, go and tell them. Go on'. With two or three young girls sitting together, he would move from 'accidentally' touching to overt sexual touching. Only on one occasion did a child stop him putting his hand up her skirt.

Paedophiles go to great lengths to put themselves within reach of children. In a well-publicised case in Brent, several men – among them Martin, Peters, and Delaney – were convicted on child abuse charges concerning several boys. Most of the victims were 'in care' in children's homes. Ken Martin had a stall selling boys' toys at the market place. He also employed one boy as an assistant and asked the parent if he could stay overnight. There were many toys at his home, the most attractive of which, including remote-control cars, he kept on a shelf above his bed.

Paedophiles often establish themselves in positions of trust which give them access to children; they seek employment in child care agencies, youth organisations and advisory services, as counsellors, or in the church or teaching professions. In one instance, an elderly retired army officer gave his name and address to a boys' public school which tried to imbue its pupils with a sense of community service, including visits to elderly and lonely people. He was a paedophile and the school obligingly sent young boys along to his country home to keep him company.

In another case, a boy was removed into care after behaving in a disturbed way. It was decided to foster him to the local vicar who subsequently turned out to be the man who was abusing the child in the first place.

A survey of schoolchildren's ideas of fairness conducted by psychologist Dr Celia Kitzinger produced a surprising result. In a questionnaire sent to 2000 children, she asked what had happened to them at school that they considered to be unfair. A hundred replied citing incidents in which teachers had made some sort of sexual advance to them.[17]

Single paedophiles often come across as nice men. Those in positions of authority will use their status in their seduction of children – a child with low self-esteem, who is possibly a poor performer at school and emotionally neglected at home, finds it very flattering if an important person demonstrates a belief that he is worth spending time on.

In counselling sessions paedophiles often admit to deliberately establishing relationships with women to gain access to their children. The growth in the numbers of marriages that break down and consequent numbers of single-parent families has produced increased opportunities for adults who sexually abuse children.

Single-parent families are often economically disadvantaged and socially isolated. A fixated paedophile may spend months building a relationship with, and may even marry, a mother to gain access to her children and children's friends. Rodney placed an advertisement in the personal column of a London paper inviting contact with a view to marriage from mothers of blue-eyed, fair-haired boys. He had eight replies and married a young mother of 18. The couple subsequently became foster-parents and fostered over 200 children. Throughout his 30 years of marriage he abused children and was not caught until he was 63 years of age.

Lack of effective support for disadvantaged families increases their vulnerability to individuals who appear to offer them emotional support and material security, but government policy also assists the paedophile more directly; the policy of keeping homeless families in bed-and-breakfast establishments for extended periods is well documented as being damaging to children's development in a number of ways. It also plays into the hands of paedophiles who tend to end up in this kind of accommodation when they are forced by Social Services to leave their own homes after detection or are released from prison.

Step-parenting is a difficult role and step-parents are a much-maligned group, both historically and in different cultures. Recent research on child sexual abuse does little to brighten the image. Writing of research in the US and the UK, Margo Wilson and Martin Daly conclude that children living with one natural parent and one step-parent are 'much likelier to be physically abused or killed than children living with two natural parents'.[18] Children living with single mothers also run a higher risk of being abused than those with two natural parents. The authors emphasise that it is a small minority of step-parents who abuse their stepchildren and point out evidence that abuse in single-parent families is most often perpetrated by male friends and acquaintances of the mothers rather than the mothers themselves.

In the book *Broken Promise – the World of Endangered Children*, Dr Eli Newberger, director of the Family Development Study at the Children's Hospital in Boston, is quoted as saying that the unemployment of males and easier employment of women, combined with the high rate of family break-down, mean that children are often left in the care of men who are not their natural fathers – 'a set-up for sexual or, for that matter, the physical exploitation of children'.[19]

The infiltration of families by some paedophiles may partly explain why we are now beginning to find more examples of men who commit incest also abusing children from outside the home.

Paedophiles do not find it hard to gain access to children; the bigger problem is how to keep a child sexually accessible and avoid detection. Gaining the child's silence is crucial. To achieve it, the rapist of children may use violence or the threat of violence. But few paedophiles choose or need to use such measures.

Their most common recourse is to create a feeling of guilt by suggesting that the child is taking part in something that is part of growing up and therefore normal, but also naughty. They will tell the child: 'You wanted this to happen', or 'You made me do this to you.' They may engage the child's sympathy – 'You and I have this very special friendship and it would hurt Daddy a lot and upset Mummy if you told'; or inspire fear of the consequences of telling – 'Mummy will run away and leave us if you tell', or 'You will be taken away and put into care if you tell', or 'They will put me in prison if you tell'.

Some men use newspaper cuttings to persuade their young victims of the danger or futility of telling, including reports of failings in state child care practice. They may show them press reports of children being taken from their families, or being handed them back again, or of a father being taken away from his children.

In the case of Robert, referred to above, the main control he imposed on the children was guilt. Despite the fact that several children were involved, no child told her parents, as far as he knew. Asked why he thought they did not tell, he replied: 'Because they had taken part'.

Once a child is made to feel partly responsible for what happens, the offender is fairly safe, even over long periods of time.

Sexually abused children can find themselves ensnared in an isolating web of both fear and affection. In many cases of incest the abusive relationship may also be the main affirmative relationship the child has, giving the paedophile a strong emotional hold. This is powerfully illustrated in the remarkable story of Liz, also in *Broken Promise*.[20] 'I wouldn't have worried too much if you had taken me away from my mother but I'd have been devastated if you'd taken me from my father.' Her father's abuse of her severely affected the course of her life. Yet he had also invested a lot of time and thought and creativity in the relationship and had made her his closest companion.

The problems of securing a child's silence can prompt an offender to continue an abusive relationship even after he is inclined to terminate it. By continuing, he can keep the child's sense of culpability and guilt alive. Once free of this regular influence, the child may be more likely to tell. All paedophiles fear the loss of control over the children they abuse. This is one reason why, against all reason, men on probation have continued to abuse particular children.

In the course of offender counselling, the author has encountered cases of the ritual abuse of children within Satanic cells. How many cells there are we do not know but there is a disquietening trend to identify any bizarre case as ritual abuse, another reflection of lack of knowledge of the offender. There are instances where the child's silence has been partly secured through a deliberate association of abuse with everyday phrases or events; for instance the stirring of a cup of tea, or the phrase, 'I'll read you a bedtime story'. In some instances the association sown in the child's mind is designed to reach into her adulthood in an attempt to secure her for the cult and obtain access to her child. In one example the association established in the child's mind was the birth of her own first baby.

Associations could be established with any phrase or any action. Impossible for an outsider to detect its relevance, it will remind the child of the abuse in which they played a part, or of the threatened consequences of revealing the abuse to an outsider.

The fact is that it is very difficult for the emotionally vulnerable child to protect him or herself against a sexually abusive adult. Obviously the difficulties children face in trying to alert others to what is happening, both in terms of the controls established by the abuser and of the tendency for the child to be disbelieved, constitute a major impediment to effective help.

Creating a climate in which children feel they are able to tell and also feel they will be effectively helped if they do tell is an important goal in freeing the child from the prison of silence that the paedophile is able to construct.

The tendency to accept the word of more powerful people against that of the less powerful works greatly to the disadvantage of the child victims of sexual abuse. They are not only disbelieved, they may also be punished for telling lies and so be pushed all the more hopelessly into a state of powerlessness and isolation. For this reason it is important to remember the message of specialists who deal with abuse victims; young children, they say, almost never lie about such matters.

There has been well-publicised and valuable pioneering work warning young children, without creating fear, against adults who might sexually abuse them. Notably, Kidscape, established by Michelle Elliott,[21] teaches children among other things the difference between good and bad touching and of the need to tell about experiences that make them uncomfortable.

At its best, the media has also done a lot to bring child sex abuse out into the open and create an atmosphere in which it can be more easily acknowledged and better understood rather than just reacted to. Many of the callers responding to a Thames Television *TV Eye* programme on child sex abuse were women prompted by the manner in which the subject was dealt with to speak for the first time of having been abused in their childhood.

The importance of encouraging a climate in which children can tell is underlined by the fact that, if they can do so after the first incident, their chances of becoming trapped are greatly reduced. Mary, aged four, playing with her older brothers and their two teenage friends, was sexually interfered with while her parents were out for an hour. On her parents' return, she immediately informed her mother that one boy had touched her and warned her not to tell. This enabled appropriate action to be taken. Mary herself felt no responsibility but, had she been unable to tell, the offence would almost certainly have recurred and she may very well have begun to develop a feeling of complicity. What enabled Mary to tell was the open and trusting relationship she had with her mother. She both felt OK about telling her and had faith in her doing something effective despite the older boy's warning.

Children who are directly encouraged to report inappropriate physical experiences with adults should be told very clearly not to inform the person they are going to 'tell on' beforehand that they intend to do so. It could place them at great risk.

Even if conditions were more auspicious, we should not simply rely on children telling or defending themselves. Parents and well-intentioned people need to be alert to the problem.

Certain kinds of behaviour or clusters of symptoms in children should awaken our concern. Abused children tend to become withdrawn or secretive. They have poor relationships with members of their peer group. They may suffer from breath-holding bouts, fainting or hysterical outbursts when under stress. They may demonstrate unusual sexual behaviour for their age or hint at such behaviour, behave disruptively or violently, or sit rocking themselves and sucking, or behave in a pseudo-mature way. Their schoolwork and general powers of concentration may also deteriorate. They may be afraid to be left alone and their eating and sleeping patterns may be disturbed. Children being abused in the home or the community may seek safety within the school, exhibiting a reluctance to leave school at the end of the day or arriving early in the morning, whereas a child being abused in a school environment would exhibit the reverse behaviour. There may be physical symptoms – itching, or soreness of, or injury to the genitals or rectum, unexplained bleeding or discharges, presence of foreign objects (young children may insert things into themselves as a result of learned behaviour), other physical injury, recurrent urinary tract infections, wetting day or night, venereal disease, and of course, pregnancy.

Teachers and other care professionals are often particularly well placed to observe a child's behaviour and they have a responsibility to take action in accordance with their professional guidelines.

But parents, relatives, neighbours and family friends also have a moral obligation to query deterioration in a child's motivation and self-image or changes in behaviour.

Offender behaviour may also alert us to the abuse of a child although offenders are good at covering their tracks. A bulletin sent to paedophiles in the UK advises that the best way to meet children is in places or activities that 'interest both of you – like in video game arcades; kids can tell if you're in there cruising for sex, or because you like to play the games. The same with sports or sporting events. You can meet kids anywhere you go that you're interested in going, and what's important about this is you've a right to be where you are. Like your own neighbourhood. You have a right to walk around, to talk to people there and get to know who's who.' The article continues: 'It's also a good idea to get to know the parents. Sometimes you can get babysitting tasks or you can take kids to places they would like going to.'

Any man whose first contact with a family is through the children should be regarded with some reservation. So should anyone who wants to spend time with or seeks opportunities to be alone with children without any very good reason, or who takes an unusual interest in children. The same goes for older boys and youths – there has been an increase in the reporting of offences by older children.

Men who encourage children to visit their homes even in groups should be treated with caution.

Without becoming paranoid, one should also be aware of relatives, family friends and acquaintances who regularly seek opportunities to be alone with the children and, more to the point, be aware of the reactions of the children to them, including their anticipation of a visit by that person, their behaviour in the person's presence and when he has left. Children may be terrified by the visits of Uncle George but feel there is no-one they can talk to. A parent may well already feel a little uneasy about George themselves without quite being able to pinpoint why. He visits the family regularly and is 'a bit over the top' in his affection for the children. The relationship may remain at the level of an ambiguous flirtatious game or, unchallenged, could develop into direct sexual contact. In such circumstances a man will use his position of trust and the incredulity that he could behave in such a way as his protection.

In the family context, some men have used a medical justification for touching children's genitals – like putting ointment on sores. But once a child can wash him or herself there really is no need to touch children in this way. Paedophiles may collect child pornography or child erotica. The collection may become very special to them and important to their sexual fantasies. They will masturbate to images of children in magazines, photos or videos as well as to fantasies of previous offences as part of the cycle that leads them to rape or sexually abuse a child. They collect books, magazine articles, newspapers, photographs, slides, films, drawings, audiotapes, videotapes, personal letters, diaries, clothing, souvenirs, toys, games, paintings.

In prison they often use holiday brochures and naturist magazines like *Health and Efficiency* for pictures of children. They have also been known to use 'Mothercare' catalogues.

A paedophile may himself take pictures of children he does not know at the beach, swimming pools, child beauty shows, in parks and at open-air events. He will be likely to use trickery, bribery or seduction to take the pictures he wants. He may lead children or their parents to believe that modelling or acting jobs might result. An advert in a magazine recently asked: 'Could your child be a model? Send three pictures; one of your child in rainwear, one in best clothes and one in nightwear.' Was it a paedophile advertisement or just a genuine appeal for a model?

Some paedophiles collect information on sexual abuse, incest and sex education and will cut pictures of children out of newspapers and paste them into scrapbooks. They may video children's programmes and make a composite of a number of them, for example sex education and school programmes, children's gymnastic programmes and *Grange Hill*. While it is not true that every paedophile collects child pornography, it is most likely that a man who does keep or collect such pornography is a paedophile.

Collecting can be a compulsive part of such men's fantasy lives and the material may be shown to children to lower their inhibitions. The possession of many photo-albums or of photos in a man's wallet of a child or children he is not related to may also signify a sexual interest in children.

The insidious nature of sexual offending against children might easily lead parents to treat any male who casts a friendly eye upon their offspring with suspicion. The exposure given to offending also produces insecurity in fathers and other men as to what is normal and abnormal in their relationships with their children. Is it wrong for a father to be naked in the home, bath the child, have children in the bath with him and so on? Men are to be encouraged to be more affectionate and to spend more time with their children rather than less. Those who have a problem with their relationship with children will know it from their fantasy life and from the kinds of thoughts they have about them. Any slight pressure on the penis can produce a partial erection. If this happens to a man when his child is sitting on his lap, it does not mean he is a paedophile. If he keeps her on his lap to stimulate the erection or puts her on his lap in the first place in order to get one, that is another thing.

In cases of incest, many wives or partners of child abusers genuinely do not know what is going under their noses. There are others who have an inkling but do not know what to do, or do not want to acknowledge the truth. They may be afraid of breaking up the family, afraid physically of their partner's anger, be economically dependent on the offender, or afraid of the public exposure they believe might ensue from reporting such an event. A few unhappy women, almost invariably themselves abused in childhood, come to take an active part in making the child sexually available to their partner and there are those who abuse children themselves.

The fears of mothers who choose not to tell place some onus on society, and more particularly the caring agencies, to provide more convincing answers to the solution of child sexual abuse within families. As things are, paedophiles are often able to argue for the partner's as well as the child's silence, and can point to press reports demonstrating that the child may be even worse off in care.

The argument of course is spurious, though care arrangements have provided quite enough incidents of secondary abuse. Child sexual abuse inflicts a heavy penalty on its victims. Liz, referred to above, was unusually resilient as the child victim of such abuse. And she had timely and successful psychotherapeutic help in early adulthood. Even so, after two broken marriages, much of her life has been an exercise in limiting the damage she in turn might inflict on others by restricting the intimacy of her relationships, even with her own children. 'I often feel I'm living life in second gear, I rarely get to the top . . . ' she says. 'Emotion is out. I've spent my life in a glass case. I can see everything outside but I can't get out and touch it.'

Failing to act effectively against child abuse, including sexual abuse, has tragic consequences not only for the child and the individual family. The costs to society go uncounted. They are to be traced in the lives of damaging and of damaged personalities, in many individuals who never achieve their full potential. Most abuse victims have to contend with a poor image of themselves and find it difficult to form successful relationships. In one study it was found that 75 per cent of convicted sadistic rapists had been sexually abused as children. In any category of rapist, one finds that at least some have been sexually abused in childhood. Boys who are sexually abused often build such behaviour into their own sexuality. They may well become offenders themselves, although it needs to be said very clearly that many do not. Girl victims commonly respond differently. Feelings of self-worth are undermined. Blame and guilt are internalised and the girl or woman may set up a life script that reinforces her poor view of herself and leads her to choose inappropriate partners. The scene is set for a repeat of the cycle.

# OBSCENE PHONE CALLS

Women are sexually offended against by men in a number of ways apart from rape – indecent exposure, frottage, indecent assault, sexual harassment in the workplace and obscene phone calls.

Such offences are routinely treated as less important than rape but they can and often do have extremely damaging consequences. Furthermore, men who commit them may be at the beginning of a career in sexual offending destined to take them on to rape and even murder. John Cannan's first known offence was, as a teenager, committing an indecent assault on a woman in a telephone box in Sutton Coldfield.

Obscene phone calls can be among the most terrifying of such experiences. Women have described obscene calls as 'mental rape' and some consider them to be as serious as physical rape. Some have been forced to move home as a result of being terrorised by obscene callers.

In making a television film about the subject for the Channel Four *Dispatches* series, producer-director Lynn Ferguson chose the title 'The Most Neglected Crime'. Research for the film included the commissioning of a Gallup Poll.

Among the film's remarkable and shocking findings was that

obscene calls are the most commonly committed crime in Britain as well as one of the most under-reported (only 25 per cent of victims report such calls to the police). Every year, nearly 2½ million women (one in 10) are subjected to at least one obscene call and most of them receive several.

The film reveals a sharp disparity between the public's attitude to obscene calls and the extreme seriousness with which they are viewed by the victims. As a rule, the victims of particular crimes, including rape, assess them to be less severe than do people who have not experienced those crimes. In some cases the assessment of the two groups matches. Only in the case of obscene phone calls do victims regard the crime as being far more severe than people who have never experienced them.

'I see this result as a clear cry for help from the victims of obscene callers for the offence to be taken far more seriously by the public and the courts,' says Lynn Ferguson.

As things stand in law, the offence is non-indictable and the maximum punishment is a fine of £400. The offence is not even against the woman who receives the call but the phone company.

The idea of the telephone as a means to a sexual encounter with someone you do not know is commercially exploited by chat-lines on which paid women respondents hold obscene conversations, and tape-lines which enable callers to listen in to taped simulated sex or 'sexy' talk.

These enterprises are damaging in a number of important ways. They reinforce the cognitive distortions that rapists and obscene callers use to justify their actions – that women like this kind of thing. Some men go on to making obscene calls because they are cheaper. Contrary to the argument that chat-lines are therapeutic and serve to reduce offending, a lot of obscene callers say they have also used chat-lines. Perhaps most dangerously, tape-lines make men angry – they are charged for at rates well above that of ordinary calls and the recordings are designed to make the men hang on for as long as possible. Several expensive minutes are spent listening to warnings of the explicitness of the impending communications.

Women who receive obscene calls often wonder if they have

been specifically targeted and even whether they perhaps did something to invite the attentions of the caller.

Many callers take their numbers at random either from the telephone book or other sources. One man has been calling several numbers three times a week for the past eight years. Some phone hundreds of numbers in the course of a year.

Jimmy gets numbers from advertising boards in shops or from classified advertisements in newspapers. He phones those that advertise clothes. If a woman replies, he will enquire about the clothes but go on to ask whether she has any underwear to sell. Some men phone up companies and ask to speak to secretaries. Some take names from newspaper captions and stories and get the numbers from directory enquiries. One man looks up the number of shops where he has seen a woman assistant he decides to target. Some callers phone women they know.

In a 1984 study of obscene phone calls, criminologist Ken Pease of the Manchester University Department of Economics and Social Policy inferred from British Crime Survey findings that at least 50 per cent of the victims of obscene calls are known to the caller. The most highly victimised groups are divorced or separated women in the early and middle years of adulthood.

Men make obscene calls for a variety of motives. They do it as part of their sexual fantasising. They may masturbate as they make the call or after the call. They do it 'for laughs', as a form of entertainment. There are those who do it for much the same reasons as the anger rapist, to offload their feelings by verbally abusing a woman, or for revenge. Some do it to exercise power and control over another individual. Yet others do it because they are too afraid to make direct contact, or out of a sense of loneliness. Some act on a combination of these motives.

The *Dispatches* programme surveyed the attitudes of 100 obscene callers who responded to an advertisement placed in the *Sunday Sport* newspaper. Among the explanations they gave for their actions were that they could not cope with relationships with women, felt they were not good-looking, or were getting revenge on women generally. Some said they felt afraid when they made the call.

Different motives produce different types of call. The friend who phones up for a game and speaks in a funny or disguised voice usually calls at a suitable hour and ensures that there are enough reassuring messages not to frighten. The aim is mutual amusement. The prankster who phones a stranger for kicks, usually dialling at random, gives no thought to the person he is phoning. He is using the other person for his own entertainment, to see if he can hook them up. Although it may not be the intention, such calls create fear and are already some way down the line to the intentionally abusive call. There are obscene callers who use the joker-call approach as a way to disguise from themselves and the recipients that they are making an abusive call.

A natural response to an obscene call is to wonder whether the caller knows where you live and will come to your home, or merely got your number by mistake or at random. Some callers deliberately foster this confusion. They are interested in using fear to exercise power and control over the recipient. These callers say, 'I know who you are.' They threaten sexual or physical abuse, or that they will snatch the children or come at night. They may describe, or pretend to describe, something in the room where the recipient is standing. This gets the woman to engage with the caller to try to find out what he knows or does not know. The longer the call lasts the more the sense of power and control grows. Six months before he was arrested for raping a woman in the Midlands, a youngster had started to make phone calls to women and children saying he would kill them. His main motive was to instil fear. He had been sexually abused within a Satanic cult and the creation of fear had become associated with his own sexual arousal.

The phone caller motivated by anger will threaten physical violence which may or may not be sexual. Of the 22 000 obscene calls made each day in Britain, 3000 are delivered with threats of extreme violence. Heavy breathers or callers who remain silent mainly aim to get a frightened reaction out of the recipient.

Calls which are immediately sexually explicit are usually the least effective, simply because the respondent almost invariably reacts by putting the phone down.

Most people who make obscene phone calls will use a confidence trick to engage the victim in conversation. They may pretend to be from a magazine or an advertising agency and doing a survey, perhaps about underwear or sexuality – anything which deceives and traps and offers opportunities for innuendo and ambiguity. Surveys give the caller an opportunity to collect some information on the person he is talking to, which he may use in a subsequent call.

Callers have professed to be in need of counselling on a sexual matter. They will say they are having trouble with a relationship and ask the recipient, as a complete stranger they will never meet, to advise them. Pretending to be conducting a police investigation is another common ploy. One couple worked together making obscene calls. The woman would phone up pretending to be a policewoman and warn that a man in the area was working through the directory making obscene phone calls. 'If he phones,' she would ask, 'will you engage him in conversation and give us time to trace the call?' The couple would then have sex together while the man made the obscene call. Other callers use threats to keep women or children listening, threatening either them or a loved one.

Angus only phones young women in hairdressing salons – he finds they stay on the line because they call their work-mates to listen in as well.

What obscene callers want essentially is a sense of progression, whether it be primarily sexual or to do with fear and power. They want to be able to say what they are going to do to the other person and what they would like her to do to them. Many hope for encouragement and to get the woman to 'talk dirty', confirming their fantasy expectations.

Their biggest turn-off is to receive no response – either silence or the shrug-off of having the phone put down. They are also put off if a man answers the phone, or if they think the operator is on the line.

Many obscene callers will just go on to try another number if they fail to get a response. Possibly because they have to try several, even many numbers, most call from their homes or places of work rather than the discomfort of a call-box and most make local calls.

Many women do in fact hang up. One obscene caller said that only once or twice in hundreds of calls had he got women to enter into a lewd conversation with him.

Despite the ratio of rebuffs, such callers maintain a fiction that women do not mind and even welcome such calls. Some will assert that they are offering excitement and adventure to women. 'It has no effect on women', 'It's probably a problem for some women, but most enjoy it', 'It's not a problem because the woman can put the phone down if she wants to', 'I think women are turned on by my calls'. 'Everyone can handle it. It's a laugh' – these are some comments of offenders. Angus claims that the staffs of hairdressing salons he phones treat his calls 'as a joke' and are therefore not disturbed by them. His need to rationalise his behaviour does not allow him to recognise that treating a threatening situation as a joke is a well-known survival strategy. If a woman tries to keep an offender talking to find out more about him, the obscene caller will take it as proof that she is a willing participant in the call.

There are men who express concern at the suggestion that they cause women distress and say they abandon a call if a woman sounds anxious. 'My calls are naughty but nice. It would be appalling to assault a woman', 'I never considered I'm frightening women', 'I haven't threatened anyone.'

Men who repeatedly make calls to a particular woman are mainly interested in exercising control and creating fear. In fact, it seems very few obscene callers carry out threats they make over the phone – at least, not with the person they are phoning.

From what offenders say, putting the receiver down without comment or pretending to be contacting the operator are winning strategies in discouraging most obscene callers. But, as with rape, the best response is whatever leaves the woman feeling most in control. If putting the phone down just leaves her feeling powerless and anxious, she may well find better ways to deal with a call of this kind.

At a level of public action, it seems high time for a reappraisal of the seriousness of this crime and for sentencing to be made more appropriate to the severity with which victims view the crime. People convicted of making such calls should also be interviewed by appropriate agencies to determine whether their offence is part of a wider pattern of abuse or disposition to abuse.

It is a reflection of the lack of seriousness accorded to obscene phone calls that the victims are made to pay to have their numbers changed, or go ex-directory or have calls to them diverted through an operator. Effectively, the recipients of obscene calls are being made to pay for being offended against, as well as for police and British Telecom inertia in investigating such calls.

Ken Pease, who along with the author was a consultant on Lynn Ferguson's film, describes obscene calls as a crime that is solvable by technology. Digital exchanges make it very easy to trace calls. It is also possible to itemise all calls – in some areas it is already established practice. Ken Pease believes that it is the responsibility of communications companies to counter crimes created by phone technology.

Apart from tracing offending calls more readily, phone companies might help by lending answer-phones for a time to aid voice identification for court purposes. Where calls are itemised, it is quite feasible to give a person a list of the calls they made and the numbers from which calls were made to them on a particular day. Phone companies ought to be pressured to meet their responsibilities.

What the *Dispatches* film exposed was the combined failure by British Telecom and the police to act, with the former being reluctant to trace calls without police involvement and the police not wishing to give the offence the kind of priority that would lead to having a trace placed.

In the making of her film Lynn Ferguson was introduced to a police officer by one of his colleagues as the journalist seeking information about obscene calls. 'Oh, do you want some then?' the officer asked her.

Women, it seems, are not only victimised by the callers in question but by a male interpretation of a crime in which the offenders are almost invariably men and the targets almost invariably women.

# PUBLIC ACTION

The rape and sexual abuse of women and children occur in the context of a range of social attitudes and ways of dealing with such offences. Reflectiveness is not the most rewarded quality in modern competitive societies and we are not highly motivated to understand why some men become rapists, even though to do so might give us the basis for preventive policies.

Society's reactions to rape range from treating it as a joke to demanding retributive punishment of offenders, the latter usually in response to a particular attack. The former reaction is used by some rapists to justify their attacks on women, while punishment without treatment serves to reinforce rather than reduce a man's propensity to attack women. What is needed is a thoroughgoing change in our whole assessment of rape and other sexual offences and of our treatment both of survivors and offenders.

By supporting campaigns and victim-support groups like Rape Crisis, writing to papers and MPs, holding discussion groups or public meetings, individuals and groups can bring pressure to bear to secure such reform.

Areas particularly worth considering are:

- How rape survivors are treated.

- The sentencing of offenders.
- The treatment of offenders.
- Better social support of vulnerable groups like one-parent families.
- Attitudes of the public, media and courts to sexual offending.


# THE RESPONSE TO SURVIVORS

Reported cases of rape in England, Scotland and Wales increased by 16 per cent from 2471 to 2855 in 1988. Whether this is due more to an increase in reporting or offending is open to speculation. Either way, most rape survivors almost certainly still face the consequences of this harrowing and life-threatening experience alone.

Isolation of the rape survivor is likely to reinforce the emotional and psychological damage she sustains. Ironically, particularly in the case of the rape and sexual abuse of male child victims, it may also help perpetuate this form of violence. Although it is important to state that many males abused in childhood do not grow up to abuse sexually, some men who rape and sexually abuse women and many of those who sexually abuse children were themselves raped or abused in childhood. While it is crucial in treatment that they must accept responsibility for their actions, it is likely that, if they had had access to timely and effective help to come to terms with the violence done to them, the damaging consequences might have been limited.

The price paid by individuals who are abused or raped is shared by society in general. Yet there seem to be no social mechanisms for recognising and responding to this fact. On the contrary, society's attitudes and legal processes help enforce the isolation of rape survivors.

Despite some police improvements, it is still common practice for women to have to report to police stations and be medically examined in the criminal setting.

There is a good case to be made for rape survivors not being interviewed in the police station at all and it is something the police themselves should have an investment in changing. Hospitals could offer a possible alternative, but in terms of considering women patients their reputation is often none too bright either. Women have experienced ordinary gynaecological examinations as insensitive or even abusive.

Perhaps the ideal would be independent or voluntary rape and sexual abuse treatment centres, under the control of the caring professions. Medical services could deal with a survivor's physical injuries and collect the medical evidence for the police. They could also give advice about pregnancy, post-sex contraceptive pills and venereal disease. A specialist worker could have a statutory responsibility to attend to the survivor's psychological needs, giving initial advice and possibly referring her to other specialists. The police, consulting with the team, could interview the woman and take evidence from her at the centre. Because she will feel supported and secure, they will in all likelihood obtain more information than otherwise and, in the case of a prosecution, probably have a far more assured witness in court. But until such a unit established its credibility, many Rape Crisis groups would still argue for centres free of any police or other statutory involvement.

Insensitivity in the handling of rape cases is not restricted to the police. Men held on remand for rape charges have been handed the deposition of their victims and other witnesses by their defence counsels. These depositions include details of the attack and evidence about the victim's sexual life. In some cases they have been used by the accused as masturbatory, fantasy material and even passed on to other prisoners. In the past the names and addresses of the rape victims could be found in these documents, especially on the medical depositions. Hopefully such information is now erased though this is often left to an individual official.

Child survivors of rape and abuse face particular difficulties in giving evidence in the intimidating court setting and in front of the adult who has exercised complete power over them. The successful lobbying for children to be able to present their evidence on video link-up is an example of the value of campaigning about such issues.

But while, as happened recently, a judge can accept the denial of sexual intercourse by a wife as mitigation for a man's sexual abuse of his child, it is clear there is still much to be done.

The police and the courts need to be cautious about misinterpreting the behaviour of the survivors of sexual offences. They risk employing the argument of the paedophile who presents the child as responsible for the adult's actions. Child survivors often demonstrate inappropriate sexual knowledge or behaviour and this is easily presented as evidence of their complicity in, if not responsibility for the offence. Invariably such behaviour in children indicates, not their sexual connivance, but that they have been subjected to abuse over a period of time.

Similarly with adults, many survivors minimise and suppress the impact of their ordeal. They may well appear composed when questioned, giving the false impression to the unwary questioner that they were not deeply affected by the experience. A wrong assumption – readily encouraged by defence lawyers – is that they were not unwilling partners.

Lenient sentences which do not reflect the enormity of the offence against the rape survivor must greatly discourage other victims of rape from enduring the court ordeal in pursuit of justice. Such judgements also reflect and tend to reinforce the male attitude that rape is not a very serious offence or that it is something caused by women. To be effective, the punishment must not only fit the crime but it must be linked to treatment of the offender if it is going to have any beneficial impact on his behaviour when he is released into the community.

# SENTENCING

There are strong calls for the punishment for rape to be made more severe – calls for long prison sentences, a return of the death sentence and even castration. Understandably, there are women who feel that castration is the most appropriate penalty. Such measures may assuage public indignation and the personal anger of some victims but they do little to diminish the incidence of rape.

Castration does not work. Rape is not primarily a sexual act but an act of abusive power and violence. Some offenders displace on to others violence done against them. Rapists who have been castrated have been known subsequently to use sticks and other implements on their victims. In prison, the abuse of sex offenders by other prisoners is fairly common and even wins some public approval. However it is also unlikely to deter them and may serve to increase the severity of their attacks on others after their release.

Sentencing is a complicated matter and needs further investigation. In America – where rape is one of the most rapidly increasing crimes of violence – it has been shown that harsher penalties deterred juries from convicting alleged rapists. In the 1970s, the US Justice Department revealed that only 51 per cent of reported rapes resulted in arrest and, of those arrested, only 60 per cent were prosecuted, of whom almost half were acquitted. Juries tended to consider the penalties excessive and therefore favoured acquittals. This realisation produced attempts to reduce sentences so as to increase conviction rates.

In the UK, by contrast, increasing pressure for harsher sentences for violent crime has resulted in parole being denied to people sentenced to more than five years for crimes of violence, except in special circumstances.

The danger of harsher sentences for rape – particularly life sentences – is that of giving the offender more reason to kill his victim, usually the only witness against him.

Another problem is the wide discrepancy in current sentencing policy. Case studies have revealed that men with similar histories, who have committed similar attacks on women, could be serving anything between four years to life sentences. Some charges have resulted in very short or even non-custodial sentences.

It is appropriate for some sex offenders to be jailed for their offences but to jail them without offering them treatment merely takes them out of circulation for a while without doing anything to deter them from offending again on their release. On the contrary, it may make them more dangerous and more skilful in evading capture.

Where sex offenders are among other kinds of prisoners, they are unlikely to face up to their offending behaviour because they will try to hide the nature of their offence out of fear of retaliation. Where they are together and have no treatment, they form their own groups and may even arrange regular meetings but the effect is to reinforce, not change their behaviour. The old saying that prisons are schools of crime is as true for sex offenders as any other group of convicts.

# TREATMENT OF OFFENDERS

Sex offenders are very much like alcoholics or inveterate gamblers in one respect – that, once a sex offender, always potentially so. They can hope to control themselves but not be cured, least of all by being locked up for a period and then released freely into the community.

On entering a part of the town where he knows there is a casino, the inveterate gambler experiences strong visual images of the place and an awakening sense of excitement. Even though he cannot afford to gamble, he tells himself he will limit his game to £50. As he starts to believe that, the visual and no sensory appeal of the casino will become stronger and the feeling of excitement intensify. Should a friend meet him and tell him he is deluded in thinking he can restrict his game, he will deny it with such conviction that a lie detector would probably show him to be telling the truth.

Having played and lost his £50, a new set of distorted thinking develops. He will tell himself that he will win the money back, or is expecting a tax rebate, or resolve to cut back on some other expenditure. He may promise himself that this is the last time.

The man is up against a complex combination of feelings, distorted thinking and sensory prompts. They can be controlled for any length of time only if he is clear that he wants them to be, if he understands how they work on him and if he has acquired techniques for exercising control. The treatment process aims at enabling the sex offender to do just that. It seeks to make him fully aware of the nature and the costs of his activities to himself and to others, gets him to accept responsibility for his actions and arms him with techniques to control his inclinations. But the choice to do so can only come from him.

In jail, where there is no treatment programme, offenders elaborate on their sexual fantasies as a result of exchanging information with each other. Some who have never thought of using weapons or implements in their attacks on women begin to build their use into their fantasies. Many agree that without help to control their tendencies, they will re-offend.

In the past such men would have been released from prison on parole, on the proviso they report to a probation officer for the duration of their parole. That might have placed at least some constraint on their behaviour on their immediate release into the community. Under the revised regulations, virtually cancelling parole, there is nothing to stop such men vanishing into the crowds on their release.

The other most striking finding to emerge from the author's counselling experience with sex offenders, in and outside prison, has been the number who have actively wanted to be helped to exercise control over themselves. It is clear that some had wanted help in adolescence but had felt there was nowhere they could safely go to get it.

The treatment of such men is still in an experimental phase but there are encouraging signs. Research in the United States shows that 80 per cent of sex offenders who have had no treatment re-offend on their release from prison. Ten to 25 per cent of those who take part in treatment programmes re-offend, but only ten per cent of those who complete a full treatment programme do so. However, there is a 50 per cent drop-out rate.

The need for the development of treatment options is also evident in the handling of child abuse cases. Until recently social workers have had no option but to remove children from families in which there is a child abuser and place them in care or, alternatively, insist that the offender vacate the home. Displacing the offender into the community in this way merely places other children at risk and it can greatly add to the trauma experienced by the child.

For this reason, the author has helped to establish the first residential centre in the community for the treatment of sex offenders against children and envisages opening up additional centres. Treatment at Gracewell Clinic, near Birmingham, is now being made part of the sentencing and release conditions imposed on child abusers. The clinic's treatment programme is beginning to find a use as an alternative to custody. In some cases, it is possible to offer treatment to the family, with wives and children being involved on a non-residential basis. A wives' group is being established, to enable the marital partners of offenders to share their experiences and identify ways forward for themselves.

One aim of treatment is to get the offender to a point where he can fully acknowledge responsibility for what he did and go on in a controlled situation to admit full responsibility to the child or children offended against. This can help free the child of guilt and so open a door in his or her mind to understanding their experience rather than just reacting to it. In some cases, where both the offenders and their families understand the full implications and reach a point at which they are able to deal with them, offenders can actually go back to their own families rather than being displaced into the community.

Gracewell is a step towards trying to tackle the problem of abusive sex at one of its sources – by offering controls to the men who abuse children. There is little else in the way of concerted treatment in the community or in prison devoted to sex offenders of any category. What there is depends very largely on the continued involvement of the individuals who run the treatment programmes.

The UK has not begun seriously to investigate the option of treatment of sex offenders – yet it is the option that holds most hope for reducing the incidence of such offences. A programme in Northern Florida allows men to be sent on a deferred sentence to a secure unit where they receive treatment for up to five years. They then appear in court to be sentenced and their progress in treatment is taken into account. While this is not necessarily the answer in this country, it demonstrates that there are different innovative ways of trying to deal with rape.

One reason for the lack of interest in treatment has probably been the expense. While the impact of rape is seen as being absorbed by the individual, the state is probably happy to leave it there. But in fact the consequences of rape and sexual assault must have severe economic as well as social repercussions.

If sexual offences affect the numbers of people we suspect, the cost must be enormous when counted in terms of work days lost, repeated attacks of anxiety, lost concentration at work, the crippled wills of some victims to make as full a contribution to society as they might, the constraint on women's freedom of movement, and so on.

Well-intentioned but unsupported or isolated attempts at treatment can be counterproductive. One offender, severely lacking in social skills, was given a week's training on how to be effective on the telephone. At the end of the week he was caught making an obscene phone call. There have also been cases of rapists being given social skills training without any other kind of treatment. Such training is only likely to increase their effectiveness as rapists.

It is all too easy to imagine you are providing sex offenders with effective treatment when you are not. One man in a group session said he would never go back to his home after treatment. Another asked him what he would do if he met another woman and found she had children in the home. His answer made it clear that he realised he would still be tempted to befriend a woman to get to her children.

Components of effective treatment would be:

- Research support for existing treatment initiatives.
- The setting up of treatment programmes within prisons.
- The introduction of specialised treatment and counselling centres in the community to which offenders can be referred on their release from prison and at which anyone worried about their sexual proclivities can be encouraged to seek advice without fear of stigma or prosecution.
- The introduction of laws under which rapists and sex offenders would have a statutory obligation to attend such centres on their release.

Treatment of the causes and contributory factors of sex offending must not stop at the treatment of offenders. Social policy has a crucial part to play, particularly in the form of support to vulnerable groups. We have already made the point about keeping single-parent families in temporary accommodation. This practice represents a failure in social policy.

We need a more energetic research programme to understand the social causes of abuse so that an effective preventive policy can be defined but we also need action now to support vulnerable families in danger of being drawn into the poverty trap and marginalised into areas of general neglect and isolation from the rest of the community.

If children are our future, as the politicians among us are so fond of saying they are, it is important for us to begin to appreciate the seriousness of abuse, both the impact on the children and the repercussions for society as a whole, and make a more committed attempt to understand and tackle the causes.

From a detection point of view, many police believe there is need for a centralised team to investigate paedophilia, child pornography and the exploitation of children in the same way that armed robbery, drugs and fraud are investigated. Such teams do not just wait for crimes to happen. They are proactive and build up a broad picture of the social environment in which crime is hatched and grows. They would actively explore paedophile networks; for instance, following up magazine advertisements that are clearly of a paedophile nature. Surely this should be the approach to all crimes of violence against the person, particularly rape, if we really do believe that people are more important than money?

# PUBLIC AND MEDIA ATTITUDES

There is already a lot of campaigning against sexually abusive attitudes to women but just listening to the way schoolboys talk about girls or considering how certain newspapers and comedians continue to confuse sex, soft pornography and rape makes it apparent how endemic such attitudes are in our culture.

Rape Crisis, the survivor counselling and campaigning organisation, has repeatedly criticised newspapers that carry rape stories on the same pages as pin-up pictures inviting readers to consider women purely as objects for sexual pleasure.

Rapists and child abusers do not have to invent justifications for their actions; they simply share attitudes prevalent in society.

The common assertion of the rapist that women want to be raped, for instance, was recently endorsed by a jury in the US when it acquitted a man of rape on the grounds that his victim was wearing a mini-skirt and therefore asking for it.

In a *Sunday Sport* article about the rape of a model, the paper printed a statement that it was unable to go into great detail of the attack because it might offend some of their family readers.

However, those who wanted to know more could phone a number, where a taped message by the raped woman would provide greater detail.

Several obscene callers have said they are able to joke about their activities in male company and can rely on other men to see the funny side. On stage and off it, rape is frequently the subject of jokes, many of which imply that women could get away if they really wanted to.

Such presentations of women, along with other forms of pornography, are part and parcel of a deeply ingrained cultural attitude that women as well as children are the property of men. The prevalence of this attitude accounts for people and organisations opposed to pornography finding themselves the target of open mockery. Mockery only succeeds as a weapon where it is assured of support. Yet many rapists and child abusers use pornography both as a stimulant in their attack cycles and as a justification. They point to it as proof of a broad social acceptance of women, and to a lesser extent children, as sexual objects – there for the taking and even inviting strangers to use them sexually.

Despite the fact that children have to be abused to produce child pornography, and that the majority of men who use it will be molesters of children, the collecting of such pornography is still seen in some quarters as rather innocent. In a recent court case, an appeal judge described the collecting of child pornography as similar to that of cigarette cards. It is the broad social acceptance of women and children as property that explains many of the grossly ill-advised court judgements in this area. In Britain the notion of rape in marriage still has to be defined as an illegal act and find acceptance as such by the courts. This would be an important step forward because it recognises the woman's right to her own body and that even within the context of a sexual relationship, she has the right to say no.

As we have noted, rapists and paedophiles are quick to integrate biased court judgements into their own armouries of rationalisations. One of the challenges of treatment is to help offenders to see such rationalisations for the excuses they are. Therapists find they are not just enabling such men to confront their own distorted thinking but that of society at large. The way they achieve this is to get the offender to see what really happens to the victim.

Counselling of male sex offenders continually brings home the parallels between their attitudes and those of people who count themselves ordinary members of society. The borderline between the paedophile and the man who confidently boasts among his peers of having 'had it off' with a schoolgirl is very fine. He also has a parallel among some socio-pathic rapists who will rape a child rather than an adult for experimental reasons, or just for the hell of it. The term 'jailbait' is used quite commonly and suggests something naughty and nice. Such values are expressed in the portrayal of children as sex objects in some commercial advertisements as well as in pornography. The popular perception of males as hunters or aggressors and women as prey or sexually subservient and wanting to be overpowered helps reinforce the complacency of the offender.

Somehow we have to establish a basis for more caring and respectful relationships between men and women, as well as between adults and children. It cannot be said clearly enough that women and children are never responsible for being raped. Men must hold themselves responsible for their own violence. At the same time, there is a social responsibility to understand why so many men resort to violence, despite the punitive sanctions against it.

Society is dangerous for women when many people believe that nice girls don't get raped; women who do get raped must ask for it; that when women say 'no' they mean 'yes'; or they like to be manhandled; or you can't rape someone who doesn't want to be raped.

Men who express such sentiments jokingly or seriously might consider the experience of Christine. She was raped in her early teens. She was returning home from a football match when she was pulled into a car by two men, one of whom knew her. They used coat-hangers to tie her up. Each raped her twice. They said they would kill her mother if she told on them. Several months later, having told no one, she was found to be suffering from gonorrhoea. She then spoke about the rape. Other after-effects she suffered over many years include:

Treatment for venereal disease.
Two D and Cs.
Removal of the right ovary.
Complete loss of pleasure in sex with her husband whom she
    married at 17.
Pain experienced in intercourse.
Intrusive thoughts about rape.
Nightmares and loss of sleep.
Divorce.
Numerous attendances at psychiatric hospitals.

# NOTES
# AND REFERENCES

1 Hicks & Platt, 'Medical Treatment for the Victim. The Development of a Rape Treatment Centre'. In M J Walker & S L Brodsky (eds), *Sexual Assault*. D C Heath & Co, Lexington, Mass, 1976.

2 *Company* magazine, September 1989.

3 R Freeman-Longo & R V Wall, 'Changing a lifetime of sexual crime', *Psychology Today*, Vol 20, No 3, March 1986, Washington DC.

4 S L Brodsky, 'Prevention of Rape: Deterrence by the Potential Victim'. In M J Walker & S L Brodsky (eds), *Sexual Assault*, as above.

5 T A Giacinti & C Tjaden, 'The crime of rape in Denver. Examination of police records'. A report, 1973.

6 The *Daily Mail*, 9th July 1986, London.

7 M Amir, *Patterns in Forcible Rape*. University of Chicago Press, 1971.

8 A N Groth, *Men Who Rape*. Plenum Press, New York, 1979. (See also *Working with Sex Abuse* by Ray Wyre, Perry-Swift Press (formerly Perry Publications), Oxford, 1987, for accounts of different types of offenders and their behaviour cycles.)

9   This story is told by Gabriela Silva Leite who formerly worked as a prostitute and is now an international spokesperson for the prostitutes' movement in Brazil and co-ordinator in ISER, the Institute for Religious Studies in Rio de Janeiro, of a campaigning and research programme related to prostitution. Her story should not be seen as confirming the notion that you cannot rape a prostitute. The notion confuses sex which the prostitute sells and what amounts to robbery with violence.

10  J V Becker *et al*, 'The effects of sexual assault on rape and intended rape victims', *Victimology, An International Journal*, Vol 7, Nos 1–4, pp 106–113, 1982.

11  There is much more to be said on this subject but techniques in building rapport are better conveyed within a training context rather than by written communication.

12  N Cager & C Schuur, *Sexual Assault: Confronting Rape in America*. Grossett & Dunlap, 1976.

13  *Men Who Molest Children*, Thames Television *TV Eye*, 12th and 19th December 1985. Two-part series on the sexual abuse of children.

14  S Creighton & P Noyes, *Child Abuse Trends in England & Wales*. NSPCC, 1989.

15  K B Lanning, in *Child Molesters – A Behavioural Analysis*. National Centre for Missing & Exploited Children, Washington, 1986. Introduces the categories 'situational' and 'preferential child molester'.

16  R Wyre, 'Why Do Men Abuse Children?' In T Tate, *Child Pornography*. Methuen, 1990.

17  R Carter, 'School for scandal', *She* magazine, October 1989.

18  R Gelles *et al*, *Child Abuse and Neglect; A Biosocial Dimension*. Aldine de Gruyter, 1988.

19  A Allsebrook & A Swift, *Broken Promise – The World of Endangered Children*; p 27. Headway/Hodder & Stoughton, Sevenoaks, 1989.

20  Ibid, p 13.

21  Kidscape, 82 Brooke Street, London SW1. Tel: 01–493–9845.